HEARING GOD

Through the Year

Dallas Willard

Compiled and edited by Jan Johnson

InterVarsity Press
Downers Grove, Illinois
Leicester, England

InterVarsity Press, USA
P.O. Box 1400, Downers Grove, IL 60515-1426, USA
World Wide Web: www.ivpress.com
E-mail: mail@ivpress.com

Inter-Varsity Press, England
38 De Montfort Street, Leicester LE1 7GP, England
World Wide Web: www.ivpbooks.com
E-mail: ivp@uccf.org.uk

InterVarsity Press®, U.S.A., is the book-publishing division of InterVarsity Christian Fellowship/USA® <www.intervarsity.org>.

Inter-Varsity Press, England, is the book-publishing division of the Universities and Colleges Christian Fellowship (formerly the Inter-Varsity Fellowship), a student movement linking Christian Unions in universities and colleges throughout the United Kingdom and the Republic of Ireland, and a member movement of the International Fellowship of Evangelical Students. For information about local and national activities write to UCCF, 38 De Montfort Street, Leicester LE1 7GP.

All Scripture quotations, unless otherwise indicated, are taken from the Holy Bible, New International Version®. NIV®. *Copyright © 1973, 1978, 1984 by International Bible Society. Used by permission of Zondervan Publishing House. Distributed in the U.K. by permission of Hodder and Stoughton Ltd. All rights reserved. "NIV" is a registered trademark of International Bible Society. UK trademark number 1448790.*

Design: Cindy Kiple
Images: Steve Lewis/Getty Images
USA ISBN 0-8308-3293-9
UK ISBN 1-84474-042-0
Printed in the United States of America ∞

Library of Congress Cataloging-in-Publication Data
Willard, Dallas, 1935-
   Hearing God through the year / Dallas Willard; compiled and edited
   by Jan Johnson.
      p. cm.—(Through the year devotionals)
   Based on the author's book, Hearing God.
   ISBN 0-8308-3293-9 (pbk.: alk. paper)
   1. Devotional calendars. I. Johnson, Jan, 1952-   II. Title.   III.
Series.
   BV4812.W55 2004
   242'.2—dc22
                                                                                                    2004004607

British Library Cataloguing in Publication Data
A catalogue record for this book is available from the British Library.

P	18	17	16	15	14	13	12	11	10	9	8	7	6	5	4	3	2	1
Y	18	17	16	15	14	13	12	11	10	09	08	07	06	05	04			

INTRODUCTION

This book is an invitation to learn to pray and listen to God more deeply so that you can conform your will to his. As you begin your journey through the year, talk to God about your motives for reading this book. Thank him that you don't have to earn his approval. Tell him about your desire to grow, and thank him for promising to meet you.

At the bottom of each page is an activity that gives you a place to start in responding to the Scripture and accompanying thoughts. That activity may be to reflect, to pray or to meditate. Responding to what God has said to you in the daily meditation is always important. Simply reading something will have little effect on you. The suggestion is just a place to start, however, and you may find yourself praying about what you reflected on, and times of meditation should usually end in prayer too.

Beyond that, you may feel led to journal. Especially if the reflection raises confusion within you, it can be helpful to write your thoughts down on paper. Also, some prayers are better written in a journal because you need to be as concrete as possible in your ideas. And sometimes God will speak to you through reflection and meditation in a way that's so downright stunning that these thoughts should be recorded and read for several days.

These devotions are not dated; you can start anywhere and move around as you please. The devotions are adapted from *Hearing God* by Dallas Willard. If you want to read more on these themes, you may want to look for his book.

You'll find a year's worth of devotions here, designed to fill six days a week. We choose to offer six rather than seven for a built-in bit of grace as circumstances do sometimes infringe on our devotional time. But you can use the seventh day to go back to some of the "pray," "journal" and "apply" suggestions you'll find at the end of the devotion.

We pray that as you read these devotions and reflect on God's word, you will be able to hear God and to allow his voice to shape your choices and encourage your heart.

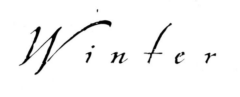

Winter

M O N D A Y *Living for God's Words*

> *Man does not live on bread alone but on every word*
> *that comes from the mouth of the LORD.*
>
> DEUTERONOMY 8:3

People are meant to live in an ongoing conversation with God, speaking and being spoken to by him. God's visits to Adam and Eve in the garden, Enoch's walks with God and the face-to-face conversations between Moses and Jehovah are all commonly regarded as highly exceptional moments in the religious history of humankind.

Aside from their obviously unique historical role, however, these moments are not meant to be exceptional at all. Rather they are examples of the normal human life God intended for us: God's indwelling his people through personal presence and fellowship. Given who we are by basic nature, we live—really live—only through God's regular speaking in our souls and thus "by every word that comes from of the mouth of God."

P R A Y : *Talk with God about the idea of having ongoing conversation. Tell God what truths you most need to hear from him regularly. Ask God to show you circumstances and places in which this conversation might occur most easily (praying, gardening, exercising or cleaning house).*

Where Am I?

The voice of my beloved!
Look, he comes leaping upon the mountains,
bounding over the hills.

SONG OF SOLOMON 2:8 NRSV

During one Sunday dinner we discussed how the pastor felt God's guidance strongly regarding how the congregation would build a badly needed new sanctuary. He testified that God *spoke* to him about things that should be done. My wife's grandmother, "Mema," seemed deep in thought as we continued to chatter along. Finally she said quietly, "I wonder why God never speaks to me like that."

We all knew that Mema had a richly interactive life with God, so her question was not a sign of weak faith or rebellion. Worse yet, we could not explain how we knew when God was speaking. I was caught up in my own experiences of the workings of God's voice, but I did not understand it. I knew only its reality, and I thoughtlessly assumed this was a functioning, intelligible fact in every believer's life.

Understanding that we hear God and how it happens is important so that our confidence that we are fully acceptable to God is not undermined.

REFLECT: *Where are you in the process of understanding how God speaks to you? If you believe you've heard God in your life, how did you know that? Why might you have discounted times God spoke to you? Ask God for guidance in pondering this.*

So Eli told Samuel, "Go and lie down, and if he calls you, say,
'Speak, LORD, for your servant is listening.'"

1 SAMUEL 3:9

In his book *Confessions,* Augustine tells how in a distraught condition he "heard from a neighboring house a voice, as of boy or girl, I know not, chanting, and oft repeating, 'Take up and read. Take up and read.'" He could remember no child's game with these words. In tears, "I arose; interpreting it to be no other than a command from God, to open the book and read the first chapter I should find." He opened to verses that addressed his exact condition (Romans 13:13-14), which was immediately transformed.

The writings of great Christians of the past such as John Calvin and William Law help us identify experiences of God's speaking, just as Eli helped Samuel. They assure us that the same Spirit who delivered the Scriptures to holy men of old speaks today in the hearts of those who gather around the written Word to teach and to learn.

REFLECT: *List people you could talk to about how they hear God in their lives. Don't dismiss those who are quiet but communicate a calm sense of the presence of God. Choose one who would be easiest to talk to and approach that person.*

THURSDAY *God, Our Teacher*

Teach me to do your will, for you are my God.
Let your good spirit lead me on a level path.

PSALM 143:10 NRSV

Hearing God. Some would say that's a presumptuous and even dangerous idea. But should we expect anything else, given the words of Scripture and the heritage of the Christian church? As Christians we stand in a millennia-long tradition of humans who have been addressed by God. The ancient Israelites heard the voice of their God speaking to them out of the midst of fire (Deuteronomy 4:33). A regular place of communion and conversational interchange between the high priest and God was established in the mercy seat over the ark of God (Exodus 25:22; Luke 1:11-21).

But the *individual* with faith among the Israelites also cried out expectantly to be taught by God (Psalm 143:10). Isaiah, who had firsthand experience of conversing with God (Isaiah 6), described the process this way: "Then you shall call, and the LORD will answer; you shall cry for help, and he will say, Here I am. . . . The LORD will guide you continually" (Isaiah 58:9, 11 NRSV).

MEDITATE: *Read Psalm 143:10 aloud and sit in the words for a few minutes. Notice how personal this phrase is: "for you are my God." Relish that. Then ask God specifically what you need to be taught from his "good spirit."*

God's Home in Us

If anyone loves me, he will obey my teaching.
My Father will love him, and we will come to him and make our home with him.

JOHN 14:23

On the evening before his crucifixion, Jesus assured his little band of followers that although he was leaving them, he would continue to show himself to all who loved him. Judas Thaddaeus then asked just the right question: *How* would this manifesting take place (John 14:22 NRSV)? Jesus replied that he and his Father would "come to them and make our home with them" (v. 23).

The abiding of the Son and the Father in the faithful heart involves more than communication or conversation, but it surely does involve these too, in a manner and measure our Lord considers to be appropriate. It is simply beyond belief that two persons so intimately related as indicated in Jesus' answer would not speak explicitly to one another. The Spirit who inhabits us is not mute, restricting himself to an occasional nudge, a brilliant image or a case of goosebumps.

MEDITATE: *Reread John 14:23 aloud slowly. Shut your eyes and savor the idea of "home." Why would God want to make a home in creatures such as us? Why would you want to have God make a home in you? What does this cause you to want to say to God?*

A Personal Relationship

God has said, "Never will I leave you; never will I forsake you."

HEBREWS 13:5

Sometimes today it seems that our personal relationship with God is treated as a long-distance arrangement in which Jesus and his Father listen to us from afar—maybe nodding and smiling. In heaven each believer has a "sin" account, which God keeps wiping clean as Christ's death pays each believer's sin bill.

But doesn't a personal relationship involve more than that? A mere benefactor, however powerful, kind and thoughtful, is not the same thing as a *friend*. Jesus says, "I have called you friends" (John 15:15) and "Look, I am with you every minute, even to the end of the age" (Matthew 28:20, paraphrase). It's reasonable to assume that this personal relationship of friends would include individualized communication—words and ideas God communicates uniquely to each friend.

MEDITATE: *Slowly reread Hebrews 13:5 or another verse printed on this page. Say it aloud to yourself and pause. What word stands out to you? Pause again. Why do you think that word stood out? What might God be trying to say to you today?*

M O N D A Y

God's Care for Individuals

Because the Lord is my shepherd, I have everything that I need!

PSALM 23:1 LB

In the last analysis nothing is more central to the practical life of the Christian than confidence in God's individual dealings with each person. The individual care of the shepherd for his sheep, of the parent for the child and of the lover for the beloved are all biblical images that have passed into the fundamental consciousness of Western humanity. They pervasively and essentially mark our art and general culture as well as our religion. Not only conservative and liberal Christians, high-church and Pentecostal, but also Christian and Jew, and even Jew and Muslim, come together in saying, "The Lord is *my* shepherd, *I* lack for nothing. *He* makes *me* lie down in green pastures, *he* leads *me* beside still waters" (Psalm 23:1-2, paraphrase).

MEDITATE: *Take each phrase of Psalm 23 (or the first few phrases), and picture how different you would be inside if you really believed it. How would your life be different if you really believed the Lord was your shepherd? If you really believed you lacked for nothing? How would you feel and how would you interact with people differently if you continually experienced green pastures and still waters with God? Don't evaluate yourself, but delight in how wonderful this would be!*

T U E S D A Y

God Invading Human Personality

You have taken off your old self with its practices and have put on the new self,
which is being renewed in knowledge in the image of its Creator.

COLOSSIANS 3:9-10

The biblical record always presents the relationship between God and the believer as a friendship or family tie rather than one person taking care of another's needs. Biblical personalities from Adam to the apostles Paul and John form a millennia-long saga of God's invading human personality and history on a one-to-one basis. There is nothing general or secondhand about the divine encounters with Abraham, Moses, Isaiah, Nehemiah, Mary or Peter.

The saga continues to our day in the lives of leaders in the spiritual life. When we consider Teresa of Ávila, Francis of Assisi, Martin Luther, George Fox, Phoebe Palmer, Frank Laubach, A. W. Tozer or Henri Nouwen, we see persons who regard personal communion *and* communication with God as life-changing episodes and as daily bread. Untold thousands of humble Christians who will never preach a sermon or have their name appear in print can testify to the same kinds of encounters with God as are manifested by the great ones in the Way.

R E F L E C T: *How do you respond to God invading human personality as a daily occurrence? How might you want God to invade your personality in greater ways?*

Singing to the God Who Speaks

[David] sang to the LORD the words of this song when the LORD
delivered him from the hand of all his enemies and from the hand of Saul.
He said: I love you, O LORD, my strength.

PSALM 18:1

When we're led personally by God, we're often swept up in a rhythm of amazement, just as David responded in song: "I love you, O LORD." Faith in a God who speaks personally to the soul is recorded in the church's hymns, sung week by week by the gathered church and day by day by Christians at work, at home, at play: "Savior, Like a Shepherd Lead Us," "He Leadeth Me" and "Guide Me, O Thou Great Jehovah." Other hymns speak about personal divine guidance and the soul's conversational communion with God, such as this chorus from C. Austin Miles's "In the Garden":

He walks with me, and He talks with me,

And He tells me I am His own,

And the joy we share as we tarry there,

None other has ever known.

PRAY: *Sit in a quiet place (a backyard swing would be ideal) and hum or sing to God a hymn or song that refers to his speaking or leading. Offer to God the other truths implied in the song. Relish the tune and how it fits the words. (Contemporary songs might include "In the Secret" or "I Love You, Lord.")*

He who forms the mountains, creates the wind,
and reveals his thoughts to man, he who turns dawn to darkness,
and treads the high places of the earth—the LORD God Almighty is his name.

AMOS 4:13

In a television interview in 1983, Dr. Ken Taylor, who produced the widely used version of the Scriptures known as *The Living Bible,* told how he had been concerned about children having a Bible that they could easily understand. According to his statement, one afternoon "God revealed" to him "the idea of a thought-for-thought translation instead of word-for-word." This idea worked so well that such versions have now been published in many languages around the world.

How do we know God is working in our thoughts? We become accustomed to interacting with a characteristic type of thought and impulse, which we learn is the moving of God upon our mind and heart. Experience teaches us the remarkable difference between when it is "just me" talking, or even "just me" quoting and discussing Scripture, and when a certain something more is taking place.

REFLECT: *In what past circumstances might God have supplied you with ideas of how to do something new or better or with more tact (love)? In what circumstances, no matter how inconsequential, do you now need some divinely inspired, mind-expanding ideas?*

Character, Not Results

> My purpose is that they may be encouraged in heart and united in love,
> so that they may have the full riches of complete understanding,
> in order that they may know the mystery of God, namely, Christ.

COLOSSIANS 2:2

We have witnessed the painful confusion of individuals who try to determine God's will and make dreadful errors. They force a desperate whim or chance event to become a sign from God. When it is not, they sink into despair.

But God did not make us to be puppets on his string. As E. Stanley Jones observed in *Victorious Living*,

> The development of character must be the primary purpose of the Father. He will *guide us, but he won't override us*. That fact should make us use with caution the method of sitting down with a pencil and a blank sheet of paper to write down the instructions dictated by God. Suppose a parent would dictate to the child everything he is to do during the day. The child would be stunted. The parent must guide in such a manner that character, capable of making right decisions for itself, is produced. God does the same. (emphasis added)

REFLECT: *Consider a decision you made that you now believe was wrong. Did it produce in you more character—integrity, simplicity, concern for others? If not, how could you now let that decision reap these rewards in you?*

God's Will and Our Will

Delight yourself in the LORD and he will give you the desires of your heart.
Commit your way to the LORD; trust in him and he will do this.

PSALM 37:4-5

Ⓦhen our children were small, they were often completely in my will as they played in the back garden, though I had not told them to do the particular things they were doing. They would still have been within my will even if they were playing in their rooms or having a snack in the kitchen.

Too often we assume that what God wants us to do automatically excludes what *we* want to do and even what *we* want *God* to do. That is not true. Generally speaking, we are in God's will whenever we are leading the kind of life God wants for us. And that leaves a lot of room for initiative on our part. God respects our initiative and ideas and thinks they are central in doing his will in our lives.

REFLECT: *Consider why we so easily assume that what God wants must not include anything we really want to do or anything we want God to do. Why is it a new thought to us that God's love includes respect for us and our desires?*

M O N D A Y

More Than Following Rules

> *For I tell you that unless your righteousness surpasses that of the Pharisees*
> *and the teachers of the law, you will certainly not enter the kingdom of heaven.*

MATTHEW 5:20

People sometimes dismiss the importance of hearing God by saying that if you just do everything God commanded, you are doing God's will. But you could do all that God explicitly commands and still not be the person God would have you be. An obsession merely with *doing* all God commands may be the very thing that rules out *being* the kind of person that he calls you to be. The watchword of the worthy servant is not mere obedience but love, from which appropriate obedience naturally flows.

There is some good in the attitude of *doing* what we are told to do by God, which amounts to the righteousness of the scribes and the Pharisees. But this severely limits spiritual growth. A life of free-hearted collaboration with Jesus and his friends in the kingdom of God surpasses that righteousness.

REFLECT: *In what situations would it be easy to do everything right and yet still miss out on loving people? What goes on in the mind of a person who is trying to do everything right? What goes on in the mind of a person who is seeking to love?*

Not God's Robots

For all who are led by the Spirit of God are children of God.

ROMANS 8:14 NRSV

Do we believe God is present only through blind faith or logical reasoning? Is a strong impression of God's presence, or seeing in hindsight that God acted within our actions beyond our powers, as experiential as God's presence gets? Although these are valid, there is more. These ideas leave our interaction with God in the realm of vague feelings, the Ouija board and superstitious conjecture.

God is also with us in a conversational relationship: he speaks with us individually as it is appropriate—which is only to be expected between persons who know one another, care about each other and are engaged in common enterprises.

When Paul said "all who are led by the Spirit of God are children of God," he wasn't saying that we are "led" by being robots or interpreters of vague impressions and signs, but that we engage God in a conversational manner that is suited to the personal relationship with God so often spoken of in the Christian community.

M E D I T A T E : *Read Romans 8:14 and try to picture the unseen spiritual reality of being led by God in a tangible way. Which scriptural image of leading fits you best: being led by the hand (Jeremiah 31:32; Hebrews 8:9); by natural phenomena (such as a cloud and fire, Exodus 13:21); by a voice (John 10:3)?*

WEDNESDAY

God's Multifaceted Ways

To these four young men God gave knowledge and understanding
of all kinds of literature and learning.
And Daniel could understand visions and dreams of all kinds.

DANIEL 1:17

What we know about guidance and the divine-human encounter from the Bible and the lives of those who have gone before us shows that *God's communications come to us in many forms.* We should expect nothing else, for this variety is appropriate to the complexity of human personality and cultural history. And God in redemption is willing to reach out to humanity in whatever ways are suitable to its fallen and weakened condition. We should look carefully at these many forms to see which ones are most suited to the kind of relationship God intends to have with his people.

REFLECT: *While God most often speaks to our thoughts especially as we read Scripture, it's important to be open to any form of communication he may use. What forms are you most open to? Least open to? (Consider such things as literature and stories, nature, visions, dreams, words of others, circumstances.)*

Motives for Hearing God

I tell you the truth, unless a kernel of wheat falls to the ground and dies,
it remains only a single seed. But if it dies, it produces many seeds.
The man who loves his life will lose it,
while the man who hates his life in this world will keep it for eternal life.

J O H N   1 2 : 2 4 - 2 5

Many people seek to hear God solely as a device for securing their own safety, comfort and righteousness. An extreme preoccupation with knowing God's will may indicate, contrary to what is often thought, that I am overconcerned with myself, not that I have a Christlike interest in the well-being of others or in the glory of God.

In *The Secret of Guidance,* Frederick B. Meyer writes, "So long as there is some thought of personal advantage, some idea of acquiring the praise and commendation of men, it will be simply impossible to find out God's purpose concerning us." Nothing will go right in our effort to hear God if this false motivation is its foundation. God simply will not cooperate. We must discover a different type of motivation for knowing God's will and listening to his voice.

M E D I T A T E : *Read John 12:24-25 slowly. Close your eyes and ponder: How does hearing God require that we die to self? That we abandon self-advancing motives? What are good motives for wanting to hear God?*

Trust in the LORD with all your heart and
lean not on your own understanding;
in all your ways acknowledge him,
and he will make your paths straight.

PROVERBS 3:5-6

There is massive testimony to and widespread faith in God's personal, guiding communication with us—far more than in blindly controlled guidance. This is not only recorded in Scripture and emblazoned upon the history of the church; it also lies at the heart of our worship services and our individualized relationships with God, and it actually serves as the basis of authority for our leaders and teachers. Only very rarely will someone profess to lead or teach the people of God on the basis of his or her education, natural talents and denominational connections alone. Credibility in any sort of spiritual leadership derives from a life in the Spirit, from the person's personal encounter and ongoing relationship with God.

MEDITATE: *Read Proverbs 3:5-6 and consider the ways you are a leader in a friendship, family, church, neighborhood or workplace. (Being a leader means that people listen to you and value your opinion regardless of whether you fill a role or hold a title.) Read the verses again and ask God to show you in what ways you need to listen for God to speak in those relationships and circumstances.*

Secret Interchanges with God

> *I will give you the treasures of darkness, riches stored in secret places,*
> *so that you may know that I am the LORD, the God of Israel,*
> *who summons you by name.*

ISAIAH 45:3

A high percentage of serious Christians (even the Babylonian king Cyrus to whom the words above are addressed) can tell of experiences of being sure God spoke to them. Yet many have never spoken of them even to their closest friends.

Robert C. McFarlane, a recent convert, was forced to take control of an insurance agency in order to save the money he had invested in it. By the third year of strain and stress, he was struggling against defeat and frustration. As he drove to his office, he was filled with a frantic urge to leave town and disappear.

Into his inner turmoil came a command: "Pull over to the curb." He did so, and these words came to him as if someone were with him in the car: "My Son had strains that you will never know, and when he had those strains he turned to me. That's what *you* should do." Robert sat at the wheel, sobbing. He drove to his office, where he faced major problems that were substantially resolved by that day's end.

PRAY: *Pray for someone who needs a secret word from the Lord. Listen to see if God has anything for you to do to help.*

M O N D A Y *Flustered Gideon*

> Gideon replied, "If now I have found favor in your eyes,
> give me a sign that it is really you talking to me.
> Please do not go away until I come back and bring my offering and set it before you."
> And the LORD said, "I will wait until you return."

JUDGES 6:17-18

Many disciples of Jesus have painful uncertainty about how hearing God's voice actually works and what its place is. Even those who believe God has addressed them may not know what to do about it. In the Bible, poor, flustered Gideon said to the Lord, "Do something to prove that you are the one who is speaking to me!"

Even if we begged God for a word, we might have so little competence in dealing with it that such a word would only add to our confusion. Perhaps for this reason God withholds the word from us. But as disciples of Jesus Christ, we must not abandon faith in our ability to hear from God. To abandon this is to abandon the reality of a personal relationship with God, and that we must not do.

MEDITATE: *Picture yourself in Gideon's place in Judges 6:15-18 (or 6:1-24 if time permits). The Midianites have been raiding your territory and an angel appears to commission you to lead your people. Are you confused, daunted, excited?*

The UFO Syndrome

> *[The Pharisees said,] "We know that God spoke to Moses,
> but as for this fellow, we don't even know where he comes from."*
>
> J O H N   9 : 2 9

For good reasons, people hesitate to believe that God is really speaking to them. If they told someone, they might be regarded as eccentric or crazy (as Jesus was regarded by the Pharisees). Like those who think they have sighted a UFO, they soon learn to keep their mouths shut.

They also fear being thought of as arrogant, as thinking they're special or "conceited because of these surpassingly great revelations" (2 Corinthians 12:7). Doubts and hesitations justifiably trouble those who feel they are spoken to by God as Gideon was. "Why is it," comedian Lily Tomlin asks, "that when we speak to God we are said to be praying but when God speaks to us we are said to be schizophrenic?"

Gideon, however, pursued the conversation with the angel of the Lord—testing the situation to see if it was real. We can do the same—think about it, wait, ask God to help us know if the speaker was himself or our own self.

R E F L E C T : *Are you sure that God has not spoken to you? What events in your past life could have been messages from God? Reflect on the details of these events.*

When in Doubt, Wait

> *I wait for the LORD, my soul waits, and in his word I put my hope.*
> *My soul waits for the Lord more than watchmen wait for the morning,*
> *more than watchmen wait for the morning.*

PSALM 130:5-6

The best work on the subject of hearing God (outside the Bible) is Frederick B. Meyer's book *The Secret of Guidance*. According to Meyer, who writes about these issues in a complete, sane and yet spiritual fashion, waiting is crucial:

> The circumstances of our daily life are to us an infallible indication of God's will, when they concur with the inward promptings of the spirit and with the Word of God. So long as they are stationary, *wait*. When you must act, they will open, and a way will be made through oceans and rivers, wastes and rocks. If you do not know what you ought to do, *stand still* until you do. (emphasis added)

MEDITATE: *Consider first the dread with which many people wait. Now read deeply Psalm 130:5-6. In place of dread, what drenches this waiting? How do you need this in your life now?*

*When he has brought out all his own, he goes on ahead of them,
and his sheep follow him because they know his voice.
But they will never follow a stranger; in fact, they will run away from him
because they do not recognize a stranger's voice.*

JOHN 10:4-5

Hearing God depends on there being a personal relationship between ourselves and God. Our failure to hear God has its deepest roots in a failure to understand and grow into a conversational relationship with God, the sort of relationship suited to friends who are mature personalities in a shared enterprise, no matter how different they may be in other respects.

It is within such a relationship that our Lord surely intends us to recognize readily his voice speaking in our hearts as occasion demands. God has made ample provision for this in order to fulfill his mission as the good shepherd, which is to bring us life, and life more abundantly. The abundance of life comes in following him, and "his sheep follow him because they know his voice" (John 10:4).

MEDITATE: *Read John 10:4-5. Close your eyes and wait for a phrase to stand out. Why is this phrase important to you?*

Freedom of Love

> *Those possessed of genuine love have God's life in them*
> *and are well acquainted with him.*
> *Those who are not have no knowledge of him, for God is love.*

1 JOHN 4:7-8, PARAPHRASE

In the movie *The Stepford Wives*, the wives are continually ecstatic about sewing and baking. When they get together they mainly trade recipes or coo over their latest triumphs in making their husbands' lives more comfortable. They are never unpleasant to anyone. A few of the wives remain on the individualistic side, but they eventually leave for a "vacation," and upon their return they focus on cleaning floors just like the rest. The surprise of the movie is that these women are all robots.

Conformity to another's wishes is not desirable, be it ever so perfect, if it is mindless or purchased at the expense of freedom and the destruction of personality. The freedom of God's love is central to how we think about God's relationship with his human creation and about what his love for us means.

REFLECT: *When we are looking for answers or making tough decisions, the fact that we are created with free choice can feel like a burden. At this point in your life, how do you feel about the freedom God is giving you?*

A Relationship of Cooperative Love

For we are God's fellow workers;
you are God's field, God's building.

1 CORINTHIANS 3:9

We must never forget that God speaks to us for the purpose of developing an intelligent, freely cooperative relationship between him and us, in which we are fellow workers or colaborers with him. God wants us to participate in the governance of his kingdom. This relationship is drenched in the maturity and richness of genuine *agape* love.

Our primary goal, then, is not just to hear the voice of God but to be mature people in a loving relationship with God. This will result in our living a *certain kind of life*—one of loving fellowship with God and those who love him. Only with this in mind will we hear God rightly.

MEDITATE: *Go over the phrase "God's fellow workers" (1 Corinthians 3:9) and personalize it. Let it sink in and compare it with the common idea that God hits people over the head with a two-by-four to get them to do what is right. Thank God that an intelligent, freely cooperative, love-drenched relationship can exist between you and him.*

M O N D A Y

Sharing the Life of God

If anyone acknowledges that Jesus is the Son of God,
God lives in him and he in God. And so we know and rely on the love God has for us.
God is love. Whoever lives in love lives in God, and God in him.

1 J O H N 4 : 15 - 16

When we love someone, we want to please him or her. This is not just to avoid trouble or gain favor; it is our way of being with them, of sharing their life and their person. Perhaps you've witnessed the gushing pleasure of a small child who is helping her or his parent. The child's little self is expanding through immersion in the life of a larger self (the parent) to which the child is lovingly abandoned. *With* his or her parent the child does big things that he or she could not undertake alone. The child would not even be interested in doing these things apart from the parent's interest, attention and affection.

PRAY: *Ask God these questions: What would it look like to immerse myself in the larger self of you? What would it look like to be lovingly abandoned to you? What do I need to be or do or decide in order to let this happen?*

A Union of Souls

I am my beloved's, and my beloved is mine.

SONG OF SOLOMON 6:3 KJV

In the union of souls in marriage—in the conscious delight and rest in one another that is the highest and most exalted relationship possible between two persons—it is not right for one person to always tell the other what to do. The beloved, who both loves and is loved, does not want to order the lover about; instead the beloved desires that the lover understand what is needed so that no orders are necessary.

And so it is in our union with God, a person both loving and beloved. God does not delight in having to always explain what his will is; he enjoys it when we understand and act upon his will. Our highest calling and opportunity in life is to love him with all our being.

REFLECT: *Are you eager for a union of souls with God or do you prefer for God to always tell you what to do? In what way might you understand his will and act on it today?*

> *Then the one who had received the one talent also came forward, saying,*
> *"Master, I knew that you were a harsh man, reaping where you did not sow,*
> *and gathering where you did not scatter seed; so I was afraid,*
> *and I went and hid your talent in the ground. Here you have what is yours."*
>
> MATTHEW 25:24-25 NRSV

Far too commonly we regard God as the man in the parable of the talents regarded his lord: "a harsh man." Such a fearful person could not "enter into the joy of [his] master" because he could not open his life to his lord or enter into his lord's life. He actually abused his lord by taking him to be interested only in his own gain, while the lord was interested in sharing his life and goods with others (Matthew 25:14-30 NRSV).

In the same way we demean God by considering him a cosmic boss who orders humans around, notes their failures and takes pleasure in seeing them jump at his command. Instead we are to be God's friends and fellow workers (2 Chronicles 20:7; John 15:13-15).

MEDITATE: *Read Matthew 25:14-30. Have you been afraid of God, or have you trusted God? When have you gone off, dug a hole and buried a precious thing? What do you think God—the joyful, kind Master—wishes you to do with it now?*

Increasing Confidence in God

Then Jesus said to the centurion,
"Go! It will be done just as you believed it would."

MATTHEW 8:13

The role of taskmaster, whether a pleased one or an angry one, is a role that God accepts only when appointed to it by our own limited understanding. He often condescends to us because our consciousness cannot rise any higher, clouded as it is by our experiences in a fallen world with our superiors (whether they be parents, bosses, kings or those who stand over us in manipulative "love"). The rule then is that things will be done "just as you believed it would." No doubt it is better that we have *some* relation to God than no relation at all!

When we come to learn how we can hear God and what divine guidance *really* is, we must be sure our ideas about God match the truth of who God is as revealed in Christ. It is difficult but important to cleanse our minds of those motives, images and concepts that brutalize the very God whom we hope to approach.

REFLECT: *How do you see God: parent, boss, king, one who stands over you in manipulative love? How would your confidence (faith) in God be affected if you saw him as a being of boundless love who invites you to become a "fellow worker"?*

Desperate to Hear

> *O God, do not keep silent;*
> *be not quiet, O God, be not still.*

PSALM 83:1

In primitive rituals such as "Bible roulette" (picking verses at random for guidance) frequently practiced by present-day believers, we see a desperate urgency to get a word from God, especially a word on what is going to happen and what we should do about it. If necessary, some people are prepared to *force* such a word from God or someone else.

Hearing God cannot be a reliable and intelligible fact of life *except* when we see his speaking as one aspect of his presence with us, of his life in us. Only our *communion* with God provides the appropriate context for *communications* between us and him. And within those communications, guidance will be given in a manner suitable to our particular lives and circumstances. It will fit into our life together with God in his earthly and heavenly family. This insight helps us in learning to discern God's voice.

REFLECT: *What methods have you used to try to get a word from God: casting fleeces, wanting something so much that you make up answers from God, going for counsel from people who will say what you want them to say? How do these attempts frustrate communion with God rather than foster it?*

Humans in Touch with God?

When the crowds saw what Paul had done, they shouted . . . ,
"The gods have come down to us in human form!" . . . [But Paul] rushed out into the crowd,
shouting, "Friends, why are you doing this? We are mortals just like you."

A C T S   1 4 : 1 1 ,   1 4 - 1 5   N R S V

The above scene portrays the common human response to people who are living in such a close relationship with God that manifestations of his presence stand out in their lives. We immediately think, "They just aren't human!" By this we mean that their experience—including their experience of God—is not like ours and perhaps that they are some special kind of people. Our experience of God could never be like theirs.

Can someone manifesting a transcendent life still be human? The humanity of Moses, David and Elijah, of Paul, Peter and Jesus Christ himself and of other riotously human women and men in the Bible and throughout church history teaches us a vital lesson: *Our humanity will not by itself prevent us from knowing and interacting with God just as they did.*

P R A Y : *Reread the last sentence. How fully do you believe that? What do you need to say to God in prayer about this? Ask God to enlarge your acceptance of this or to enlarge your understanding of it.*

M O N D A Y   *No "Once upon a Time"*

All these people were still living by faith when they died.
They did not receive the things promised. . . .
They were longing for a better country—a heavenly one.

HEBREWS 11:13, 16

We must study the Bible with the assumption that the experiences recorded there are basically the same as ours would have been if we had been there. The Bible characters felt very much as we would have if we had experienced those things. They were real people who hurt and laughed as we do. Like us, they longed for what they could not see.

Unless this comes home to us, the experiences recorded in the Bible will remain unreal to us. We will not genuinely believe the Bible or find its contents to be real because it will have no experiential meaning for us.

REFLECT: *Consider your favorite Bible character(s). What frustration and despair might they have experienced? What surprises might have astonished them? How would you have felt in their circumstances? If they encountered God in a tangible way (such as Moses at the burning bush and Jacob wrestling the "man"), how would you have felt if you had been them? Would you have thought of it every night before you went to sleep? Pray about not viewing Bible characters as fantasy characters but as people who bled and did not have perfect faith.*

Missing the Point

> *You have never heard [the Father's] voice nor seen his form,*
> *nor does his word dwell in you, for you do not believe the one he sent.*
> *You diligently study the Scriptures because you think that by them you possess eternal life.*
> *These are the Scriptures that testify about me, yet you refuse to come to me to have life.*

J O H N   5 : 3 7 - 4 0

When we read the Bible as if the persons in the Bible didn't struggle as we do, it becomes simply a book of doctrine. It becomes an abstract truth about God that people can search endlessly without encountering God himself or hearing his voice (John 5:39). How can people miss the point this way? In *The Root of the Righteous*, A. W. Tozer remarked:

> It is possible to be instructed in the rudiments of the faith and still have no real understanding of the whole thing. It is possible to become expert in Bible doctrine and not have spiritual illumination, with the result that a veil remains over the mind, preventing it from apprehending the truth in its spiritual essence.

PRAY: *Seek God in prayer, asking him to enlighten the eyes of your heart so that his word abides in you. Implore God to keep you from searching endlessly without encountering God himself or from studying without receiving spiritual illumination.*

Bible Boredom

The life-maps of GOD are right, showing the way to joy.

PSALM 19:8 *THE MESSAGE*

When we do not understand the experience of biblical characters in terms of our own experience, we may stop reading the Bible. Or we take it in regular doses, choking it down like medicine, because someone told us that it would be good for us—though we really do not find it to be so.

The open secret of many "Bible-believing" churches is that only a small percentage of their members study the Bible with the degree of *interest, intelligence* or *joy* that they bring to reading their favorite newspaper or magazine. Based upon considerable experience, I believe this is primarily because they do not know and are not taught how to understand the experience of biblical characters in terms of their own experience.

REFLECT: *Recall times (if any) when you have read the Bible with interest, intelligence or joy. What factors were present? What are some steps you could take to experience Bible reading this way? (You might want to discuss this with a friend as you reflect on it.)*

What If?

> *For we do not have a high priest who is unable*
> *to sympathize with our weaknesses,*
> *but we have one who in every respect has been*
> *tested as we are, yet without sin.*
>
> HEBREWS 4:15 NRSV

The Bible teaches that we are to understand it in terms of our experience when it says that Paul and Barnabas were human beings like us (Acts 14:15) and that Jesus knows how we feel because he "has been tested as we are." Their experience was substantially like our own.

To hear God's voice we must observe how his word came to people in the Scriptures and prayerfully but boldly use our God-given imaginations as we read their stories. What would it be like if *we* were Moses standing by the bush (Exodus 3:2), little Samuel lying in his darkened room (1 Samuel 3:3-7), Ananias receiving his vision about Paul (Acts 9:11) or Peter on his rooftop (Acts 10:10)? We must pray for the faith that would enable us to believe that *such things could happen to us.* Only then will we be able to recognize, accept and dwell in them when they come.

M E D I T A T E : *Read one of the references about Moses, Samuel, Ananias or Peter and the verses around it. What would you have seen, heard, tasted, touched or smelled? In what ways would you never have been the same after this experience?*

FRIDAY *How Important Am I?*

> Don't you know that you yourselves are God's temple
> and that God's Spirit lives in you?

1 CORINTHIANS 3:16

In the movie *Gandhi*, the young Indian lawyer and a white clergyman are walking together on a boardwalk in South Africa, contrary to its laws at the time. Some brutish-looking young white men threaten to harm them, but the ringleader's mother calls from a window and commands him to go about his business.

When the clergyman exclaims over their good luck, Gandhi comments, "I thought you were a man of God." The clergyman replies, "I am, but I don't believe he plans his day around me!"

A cute point, but beneath it lie beliefs that make it difficult to take seriously the possibility of divine guidance. One of those beliefs is that we are not important to God. But we were important enough for God to give his Son's life for us and to choose to inhabit us as living temples. Obviously, then, we are important enough for God to guide us and speak to us whenever it's appropriate.

PRAY: *Consider what sort of God would create you, sacrifice enormously for you, choose to inhabit you, but refuse to speak to you? Pray, thanking God for being such a relational God, who chooses to sacrifice for you, inhabit you and have an interactive life with you.*

God's Greatness

> *Now to him who is able to do immeasurably more than all we ask or imagine,*
> *according to his power that is at work within us, to him be glory in*
> *the church and in Christ Jesus throughout all generations, for ever and ever!*

E P H E S I A N S   3 : 2 0 - 2 1

Can a normal person like me really be capable of having the same kinds of experiences as did Elijah or Paul? Who am I to put myself in the place of these great ones? Who am I even to suppose that God might guide me or speak to me, much less that my experience should be like that of Moses or Elisha?

Such questions may seem to honor the greatness of God, but in fact they contradict what God has taught about himself in the Bible and in the person of Christ. *God's greatness is precisely what allows him to pay close attention to me or anyone and everyone else, as he chooses.* God's greatness is shown in his ability to work *within* anyone.

M E D I T A T E : *Read again Ephesians 3:20-21. What word or phrase stands out to you? "Immeasurably more"? "Ask or imagine"? "Power at work within us"? Delight in the wonder of these ideas and then respond to God in prayer.*

44

M O N D A Y *Beyond Our Inadequacies*

> *The cry of the Israelites has reached me, and I have*
> *seen the way the Egyptians are oppressing them. So now, go.*
> *I am sending you to Pharaoh to bring my people the Israelites out of Egypt.*

EXODUS 3:9-10

Those to whom God spoke, such as Moses and Gideon, often pleaded unworthiness or inadequacy. While such responses are appropriate in a sense, they are also beside the point. They are irrelevant, because God does not speak to us to indicate we are worthy of flattery or more adequate than others.

God's speaking to us does not make us *important*. Just as when he spoke to the ancient people of Israel, his speaking to us gives us greater *opportunity* to do good and greater *responsibility* for the care of others. God speaks to us because he wants to join him in some purpose of advancing the kingdom of God here on earth.

REFLECT: *Read Exodus 3:9-10 and notice how the tender heart of God is broken. Notice God's invitation to Moses to join him in an enormously redemptive purpose. Then read Exodus 3:11-4:13 and note Moses' protests of inadequacy. Where in your life are you lodging protests, complaining and dragging your feet in following God because you're focusing on your inadequacies rather than on God's desire to advance the kingdom of love here on earth? What would be helpful for you to pray?*

Sitting down, Jesus called the Twelve and said,
"If anyone wants to be first, he must be the very last, and the servant of all."
He took a little child and had him stand among them. Taking him in his arms,
he said to them, "Whoever welcomes one of these little children in my name welcomes me; and
whoever welcomes me does not welcome me but the one who sent me."

MARK 9:35-37

If a high government official called us, we might think that would make us important. Similar thoughts may be stirred when we think about God speaking to us. *Wow, I've arrived!* But such inferences can shut us off from the individualized word of God. If God's conversational walk with us makes us think we are people of great importance, his guidance will certainly be withdrawn. For we cannot be trusted with it. In the kingdom of God, those who exalt themselves will be abased, and pride comes before a fall. If God speaks to us, he does so to help us become a part of what he is doing in the world to care for and guide others.

MEDITATE: *Read Mark 9:35-37. Imagine yourself as a small child who is content to tag along with God and be a small part of what God is doing. How would that childlike perspective make you an ideal servant in the purposes of God?*

WEDNESDAY *Humility in Hearing*

When pride comes, then comes disgrace, but with humility comes wisdom.

PROVERBS 11:2

Moses may be the all-time record holder for lengthy conversations with God. But he was also one of the least presumptuous human beings who ever walked the earth: "Moses was very humble, more so than anyone else on the face of the earth" (Numbers 12:3). Certainly a connection existed between his meekness and his close working and talking relationship with God.

In seeking and receiving God's word to us today, we must also seek and receive the *grace of humility.* God will gladly give it to us if, trusting and waiting on him to act, we refrain from

- *pretending* we are what we know we are not;
- *presuming* a favorable position for ourselves in any respect;
- *pushing* or trying to override the will of others in our context.

This is a fail-safe recipe for humility: Never push, never presume, never pretend.

PRAY: *Ask for the guidance of the Holy Spirit. Then ask God: Where do I pretend to be smarter or kinder or more clever than I am? Where do I presume to know more than others or to deserve better treatment? When am I often pushy? Confess this lack of humility to God and ask him for guidance in learning to put all your trust in him.*

He leads the humble in what is right, and teaches the humble his way.

PSALM 25:9 NRSV

While some assume that doing God's will must be distasteful—Gulp! Not *my* will, but *Thy* will!—the humble person is open to God's will being the best possible future. In *George Mueller of Bristol and His Witness to a Prayer-Hearing God,* A. T. Pierson comments on Psalm 25:9 and the essential role of humility in receiving guidance from God:

> [Note] a double emphasis upon *meekness* as a condition of guidance. Where this holy habit exists, there is an *inward* recognition and choice [to do] the will of God. God guides by *swaying the judgment.* To wait before God in readiness to see which way [seems right] is a frame of mind and heart in which one is fit to be guided. God touches the scales and makes the balance to sway as he will. *But our hands must be off the scales,* otherwise we need expect no [ideas from God].

Humility is essential to keeping our hands off the scales and remaining open to the heart of God.

REFLECT: *How does believing that God's will is the best of all possible futures help you stay open to hearing whatever God may say to you? What do you honestly believe about God's will being the best of all possible futures?*

F R I D A Y

Pride goes before destruction, a haughty spirit before a fall.

PROVERBS 16:18

When God speaks to us *it does not prove that we are right or even that we are good.* In fact we may have misunderstood what God said. The infallibility of God the speaker does not guarantee our infallible reception. However, phrases such as "God told me" or "the Lord led me" are commonly used to prove that "I am right," *"My ideas* are right" or *"you* should follow *me."* No such claim is automatically justified.

So if a conversational walk with God does not guarantee my always being right, what is the use of it? Why should we attempt to hear God if it won't ensure that we're on the right track? God's purposes in speaking to us are *not* to support our roles or to make sure that we are right. God speaks to us to give us *opportunities* to be and to do good and *responsibilities* to care for and guide others.

PRAY: *Ask God to show you the parts of your inner self that want to be right about how things are done or how relationships should work. When do you most often use the word* should? *In what areas are you sure you know much more than others? Then ask God to help you surrender to his divine rightness.*

Even though I walk through the valley of the shadow of death,
I will fear no evil, for you are with me; your rod and your staff, they comfort me.

PSALM 23:4

Once while detained in London I spent time meditating and praying in Westminster Cathedral. The building's vast, obscure interior impresses me with the nearness of God. In front of the cathedral is a square with benches. Off to one side is a McDonald's, where London's street people come to sleep safely in the morning sun and to glean scraps of haute cuisine left by those who dine with Ronald. I watched a blond, middle-aged woman several times as she slept with children and pigeons flocking around her. While she showed the marks of street life, she looked very much like any woman at the center of a happy family. I thought, *Whose daughter is she? Whose sister or mother or neighbor? And here she is, alone!*

After my experience of the nearness of God in the cathedral, her aloneness stunned me. But perhaps at other times she stepped into the cathedral so that in the valley of deathly shadows she found nothing to fear. Why? Because "you are with me" (Psalm 23:4).

REFLECT: *Where are the places or times when you sense the nearness of God even though you may be alone? Consider how this nurtures you and when you might next go there.*

M O N D A Y

Then what can separate us from the love of Christ?
Can affliction or hardship? Can persecution, hunger, nakedness, danger, or sword? . . .
Throughout it all, overwhelming victory is ours through him who loved us.
For I am convinced that there is nothing in death or life,
in the realm of spirits or superhuman powers, in the world as it is or the world as it shall be,
in the forces of the universe, in heights or depths—
nothing in all creation that can separate us from the love of God in Christ Jesus our Lord.

ROMANS 8:35, 37-39 NEB

When our first child was born, I realized painfully that this beautiful little creature was separate from me and nothing I could do would shelter him from his aloneness in the face of time, brutal events, others' meanness, his own wrong choices, the decay of his body and, finally, death.

That would be the last word on the subject, except for God. He is able to penetrate and intertwine himself within the fibers of the human self in such a way that those who are enveloped in his loving companionship will never be alone.

MEDITATE: *Read Romans 8:35, 37-39. Read it again, inserting whatever separates you from Christ into the list after* sword *(perhaps loneliness, rejection, uselessness). Read the last verse aloud with as much power as you can muster.*

Presence, Not Presents

Be content with what you have; for he has said,
"I will never leave you or forsake you."
So we can say with confidence,
"The Lord is my helper; I will not be afraid.
What can anyone do to me?"

HEBREWS 13:5-6 NRSV

We seek the person and presence of God partly for how it benefits our life circumstances. Indeed, the presence of God is a place to hide from the intrigues of people (Psalm 27:5, 31:20; 32:7).

Yet trying to control our circumstances by means of God's presence is not what we rest in as disciples of Jesus. In God we are content and count with confidence on the Lord (Hebrews 13:5-6). The promise is not that God will never allow any evil to come to us, but that no matter what befalls us, we are still beyond genuine harm because God remains with us and his presence is enough by itself. Our contentment lies not in God's presents to us but in the presence of the One whose presents they are.

PRAY: *Consider this phrase: God remains with us and his presence is enough by itself. If God were to ask you, "Am I enough?" what would be your honest answer? Talk to God about this. If you wish, ask God what the next step would be in letting him be enough.*

God with Us

Remember, I am with you always, to the end of the age

MATTHEW 28:20 NRSV

Loneliness is loose upon the landscape. It haunts the penthouse and the barren apartment, the executive suite and the assembly line, the cocktail bar and the city streets. It is, as Mother Teresa of Calcutta once said, the leprosy of the modern world. Lonely people live apart from God, "without hope and without God in the world" (Ephesians 2:12). Their experiences of alienation are rooted in alienation from God.

It does not have to be so. St. Augustine has written in *The City of God* that when we come to our final home, "there we shall rest and see, see and love, love and praise." It is this for which the human soul was made. As the Westminster Shorter Catechism affirms, it is our temporal and eternal calling: "Man's chief end is to glorify God and enjoy him forever."

PRAY: *Pray this portion of the "Breastplate of St. Patrick" and notice which phrases stand out to you most. Linger in those phrases, tasting them in joy.*

> *Christ be with me, Christ within me, Christ behind me, Christ before me,*
> *Christ beside me, Christ to win me, Christ to comfort and restore me.*
> *Christ beneath me, Christ above me, Christ in quiet, Christ in danger,*
> *Christ in hearts of all that love me, Christ in mouth of friend and stranger.*

Reigning with God

> *As you come to him, the living Stone—rejected by men but*
> *chosen by God and precious to him—you also, like living stones,*
> *are being built into a spiritual house to be a holy priesthood,*
> *offering spiritual sacrifices acceptable to God through Jesus Christ.*

1 PETER 2:4-5

Life with God is a life in which one is never alone. We have a "with" relationship to God, in which we are forever rid of isolation and loneliness. One of the concrete ways of understanding this is through the intriguing suggestions in these verses: "You shall be for me a priestly kingdom and a holy nation" (Exodus 19:6 NRSV); "To him who loves us and freed us from our sins by his blood, and made us to be a kingdom, priests serving his God and Father, to him be glory and dominion forever and ever" (Revelation 1:5-6 NRSV).

God calls us to a direct and fully self-conscious, personal relationship with him (as priests) in which we share responsibility with him in the exercise of his authority (as kings).

R E F L E C T : *How do you respond to the idea that part of our life with God involves sharing responsibility with God in exercising authority? What do you need to do to become equipped for such a role?*

F R I D A Y   *Isn't God Everywhere?*

> *If I go up to the heavens, you are there;*
> *if I make my bed in the depths, you are there.*
> *If I rise on the wings of the dawn, if I settle on the far side of the sea,*
> *even there your hand will guide me, your right hand will hold me fast.*

PSALM 139:8-10

Many people do believe that God is with them—perhaps because of past experiences, others' say-so or reasoning that points to this. But is that all? Do we have no awareness of God's being here with us now? Do we have no evidence of God's action in or around us?

Although belief in God's omnipresence is essential, the human heart can never be content to simply have blind faith that God is present. This cannot be an adequate foundation for sustained spiritual growth. There is much more to know and receive. Otherwise they will never enter into their capacities as kings and priests, never "reign in life through the one man, Jesus Christ" (Romans 5:17).

MEDITATE: *Read Psalm 139:8-10 and ask yourself, Do I believe God's presence with me at all times: because the Bible says so? Because others believe it? Because reasoning points to this? Because I have an awareness of God being here with me? Because I've seen evidence of God's action in or around me?*

A Corporate Presence

Again, I tell you that if two of you on earth agree about anything you ask for,
it will be done for you by my Father in heaven.
For where two or three come together in my name, there am I with them.

MATTHEW 18:19-20

Beyond simple faith in God's omnipresence, we sometimes have a vague but powerful sense, feeling or impression of God's presence. We need considerable experience in order to learn how to accurately recognize this and assess the meanings of such impressions. Yet a sense of God's presence is frequently verified through the judgment of several individual members of the group. Different people simultaneously sense that certain things are to be done—that God is here and is moving in that direction.

This corporate sensing is a well-known phenomenon. Experienced ministers and laypersons frequently find they have synchronized their activities unerringly in a meeting or other form of service through their sense of God's presence and what God intends for the particular occasion. It is something they come to expect and to rely upon.

PRAY: *Consider a time when a certain community of believers in which you were involved (church, small group, lunch group) sensed God's presence moving. Especially if you did not do so then, thank God now that he makes his divine presence sensed and known, not only for individuals but also for entire groups.*

M O N D A Y *Sensing God's Gaze*

> *From heaven the LORD looks down and sees all mankind;*
> *from his dwelling place he watches all who live on earth—*
> *he who forms the hearts of all, who considers everything they do.*

PSALM 33:13-15

A strong sense of a person's presence occurs at a purely human level. We may have the distinct impression that someone is looking at us or listening to us, only to later learn that in fact a certain person was looking intently at us or listening to us. Or someone attracts your attention (across a large hall, for example) merely by staring intently at the back of your head. Some people seem more sensitive than others to such things, just as some have better eyesight or more acute hearing than others have.

It is clear enough that one person's conscious concentration upon another frequently evokes a reciprocal awareness. Since this is known to be true among human beings, we should not be surprised that God's attention to us should result in our reciprocal awareness of his presence.

MEDITATE: *Read Psalm 33:13-15. Imagine places and situations in your life where you could draw comfort and strength from the truth that God watches you there and does not take his eyes off you. How would you like God to form your heart in those places or situations?*

Effects of God's Presence

And God spoke to Israel in a vision at night and said, "Jacob! Jacob!"
"Here I am," he replied.

GENESIS 46:2

Sometimes the sense of "God with us" becomes distinct. My brother, J. I. Willard, served as a minister for over thirty years, but his entry into ministry came through intense struggles.

One evening he faced a major decision that had to be made the next day. He prayed into the night, falling asleep only to be awakened as the "room lit up with the glory of God. I saw a figure. I did not see a face, but I recognized it to be the person of Christ. I felt a hand on my shoulder, and I heard a voice that said, 'Feed my sheep.'"

The presence of God almost overwhelmed his consciousness, and it also transformed various aspects of his personality. He was suddenly living in the study of the Bible, memorizing without trying to do so, even though his days were spent in hard physical labor. His painful addiction to tobacco was removed without asking. The "aroma" of that room full of God's presence has stayed with him ever since. Many others would testify that it is so.

REFLECT: *Notice which areas of J. I. Willard's life were affected by his experience. How did this equip him to move forward as aging Jacob's experience equipped him to go on to Egypt?*

The God Who Multiplies

Five of you will chase a hundred, and a hundred of you will chase ten thousand,
and your enemies will fall by the sword before you.

LEVITICUS 26:8

The sense of God's presence is sometimes accompanied in Christian experience by extraordinary events or powerful effects not attributable to merely natural causes. The mark of the working of God's Spirit with us is the *incommensurability* of the effects with our merely human powers. A hundred soldiers will be cornered by only five, and ten thousand will run in fear from only one hundred. The working of God's Spirit produces disproportionate results that do not make sense humanly. The outcome is beyond human logic to understand or natural powers to accomplish. Such humanly unaccountable effects fit into, and even certify, the principles and purposes of the rule of God in human history, as manifested in the works of Christ.

REFLECT: *Read Leviticus 26:1-13. What commands does God issue in order for supernatural results to occur? What unexplainable results would follow? What would Israel's relationship with God look like (vv. 11-13)? Reread the verses that begin with "I will . . ." (vv. 4, 6, 9, 11, 12). Which of these promises would you have cherished most if you had been one of the participating Israelites? Why?*

Unexplainable Results

Taking the five loaves and the two fish and looking up to heaven,
he gave thanks and broke them. Then he gave them to the disciples to set before the people.
They all ate and were satisfied, and the disciples picked up
twelve basketfuls of broken pieces that were left over.

LUKE 9:16-17

After many years of successful ministry, Dwight Lyman Moody had this experience, recorded in A. P. Fitt's *The Shorter Life of D. L. Moody:*

> I seldom refer to it, it is almost too sacred an experience to name. . . . .
> I can only say God revealed Himself to me, and I had such an experience of His love that I had to ask Him to stay His hand. I went to preaching again. The sermons were not different; I did not present any new truths; and yet hundreds were converted. I would not now be placed back where I was before that blessed experience if you should give me all the world.

Moody was a constant source of wonder because the effects of his ministry were so disproportionate with his limited personal qualities. He was ordinary looking, quite uncultured and uneducated—even uncouth and crude to many—and not ordained by any ecclesiastical group.

PRAY: *Come to God, acknowledging his presence, offering what time, energy or money you have (five loaves and two fish). Ask God to multiply it as appropriate.*

F R I D A Y   *Beyond the Natural*

> *For those who live according to the flesh set their minds on the things of the flesh,*
> *but those who live according to the Spirit set their minds on the things of the Spirit. . . .*
> *But you are not in the flesh; you are in the Spirit,*
> *since the Spirit of God dwells in you.*

ROMANS 8:5, 9 NRSV

Contrary to nature, Abraham fathered Isaac—the son of promise and spirit—with Sarah. It was achieved through the energy of the Spirit, who was beyond Abraham and Sarah. At an earlier time Abraham and Hagar quite naturally begat Ishmael through the mere energies of their bodies (Galatians 4:22-28).

A life with effects beyond the natural (flesh) always depends upon intimate interactions between us and God, who is therefore present. These interactions occur in those who "set their minds on the things of the Spirit." Then the "Spirit of God dwells in [them]" and supernatural results come to pass.

MEDITATE: *Read Romans 8:5-11 aloud slowly. In what situation are you living by "the flesh" (natural abilities)? If you were living by the Spirit instead, how would things be different? How would you pray differently about people involved in that situation? How would you study differently or worship differently? What might you need to confess?*

God Acting with Us

> When they arrived, they called the church together and related all that
> God had done with them, and how he had opened a door of faith for the Gentiles.
>
> ACTS 14:27 NRSV

When Paul and Barnabas set out on their first missionary journey, they moved in a power that was beyond themselves (Acts 13—14). The result was an astonishing series of events, establishing communities of believers in Christ throughout central Asia Minor.

When they returned to their home in Syrian Antioch they brought the community of believers together and matter-of-factly reported everything that God had done *with them*. No one doubted God's presence with them because he had energized their activities with a power beyond their own. The fulfillment of Jesus' words—"he abides with you, and he will be in you" (John 14:17 NRSV)—was the most obvious fact of their lives.

PRAY: *If you do want this to happen, pray that God will act with you, doing the great things he wants done. Ask that the pattern of your life will be one of God abiding in you. If you're not sure you really want this to happen, ask God to show you what more is needed within you.*

MONDAY
The Secret Conversation of the Soul

> *"Come," my heart says, "seek his face!" Your face, LORD, do I seek.*
>
> PSALM 27:8 NRSV

God is personal, and God wants to talk with us. So part of the ongoing relationship between human beings and God is the practice of the presence of God that Brother Lawrence wrote about:

> I make it my business to persevere in his Holy presence, wherein I keep myself by a simple attention and a general fond regard to God, which I may call an ACTUAL PRESENCE of God; or, to speak better, an habitual, silent, and secret conversation of the soul with God, which often causes me joys and raptures inwardly, and sometimes also outwardly, so great that I am forced to use means to moderate them and prevent their appearance to others. *(The Practice of the Presence of God)*

In this way we are friends of God and also priests because we participate fully in the kingdom of God, working shoulder to shoulder with our Lord.

REFLECT: *How do you respond to the idea that "God is personal, and God wants to talk with us"? During what daily activities would you be able to incorporate that ongoing "secret conversation of the soul with God"?*

Two Types of Guidance

I will instruct you and teach you in the way you should go;
I will counsel you and watch over you.
Do not be like the horse or the mule, which have no understanding
but must be controlled by bit and bridle or they will not come to you.

PSALM 32:8-9

One type of guidance is mechanical, such as driving a car or operating a remote-control model airplane. We cause an object to move in a way we prefer. The second type of guidance is personal. When we guide other people, we take into account their thinking power and preferences. Ideally we advise them to use their mind fully and do not coerce their will.

God generally deals with nonpersonal creation mechanically, but he guides humans by communicating intentions and thoughts. God addresses the person. So in Psalm 32:9 we are admonished not to be like a horse or a mule without understanding, but to be led by—guided by—reasonable, intelligible communication from God.

PRAY: *Reflect to God about the truths that he doesn't guide us mechanically (if A happens, people should always do B) and that he guides us with reasonable, intelligible communication ("I will instruct you . . ."). Tell God how you respond to being instructed and taught by him.*

The Lord called to him in a vision, "Ananias!"
"Yes, Lord," he answered.

ACTS 9:10

One way God communicates with us is through a voice or in words addressed to—or even through—us. In Acts 9:10-16 the Lord appeared to Ananias and told him that he should go and speak to Paul, who was praying and fasting after having been struck down on the road to Damascus. According to the biblical record, such things happened to Paul over and over. When he was about to go into Bithynia, the Holy Spirit would not let him go. As he waited at Troas, he had a dream that instead of staying in his home territory in Asia Minor, he should take a radically new direction and enter Europe. In the dream a man from Macedonia called to him, saying, "Come over . . . and help us" (Acts 16:6-9).

None of these communications were matters of strong impressions or hindsight of supernatural events. The primary manner of communication from God to humankind is the Word of God, or God's speaking to us.

MEDITATE: *Read Acts 9:10-16. Note how God addressed Ananias three times and Ananias answered twice with immediacy. Picture God calling to you in a vision and your answering without hesitation, "Yes, Lord!" because you are sure of who is speaking to you.*

God Speaking to the Church

When you come together, everyone has a hymn, or a word of instruction,
a revelation, a tongue or an interpretation.
All of these must be done for the strengthening of the church.

1 CORINTHIANS 14:26

Purposeful, intelligent communications in words seem to have been normal experiences for early Christians. In the advice given on how meetings of the church were supposed to proceed, it is assumed that numerous people in the congregation will have some kind of communication from God which they will share with the others in the group—a hymn, a teaching, a revelation, a tongue or an interpretation (1 Corinthians 14:26).

The ancient prophecy of Joel was fulfilled in the early church: "Your sons and daughters will prophesy, your young men will see visions, your old men will dream dreams" (Acts 2:17; compare Joel 2:28-32). The wish of Moses "that all the Lord's people were prophets and that the LORD would put his Spirit on them" (Numbers 11:29) is granted in the church of Jesus Christ when it functions as its Lord intended.

PRAY: *Hold your church newsletter or directory in your hand. Pray for individuals in your church. Pray that during the next gathering God will speak clearly to people. Sit and listen. Is God saying anything to you about something you need to do before, during or after that gathering?*

Knowing God's Thoughts

> *Those who are spiritual discern all things,*
> *and they are themselves subject to no one else's scrutiny.*
> *"For who has known the mind of the Lord so as to instruct him?"*
> *But we have the mind of Christ.*
>
> 1 CORINTHIANS 2:15-16 NRSV

Besides speaking through people and using words, God communicates intentions and thoughts another way to those who are with him. Here we come to know what God wants us to understand through immersion with him in his work. We understand what he is doing so well that we often *know exactly what he is thinking and intending to do.* I believe that this is a great part of the condition described by the apostle Paul as "having the mind of Christ."

In this way, the recipient of God's communication takes a more active role. This way is common among those who are most mature in God's family or kingdom.

REFLECT: *Make a quick list of the thoughts and intentions of God that you know about from Scripture and the way you've seen holy people live. (It will be interesting to see what comes to your mind first!) Then go over the list and refine it, looking through passages such as Colossians 3:1-17. Finish by asking God to make his thoughts and intentions living and active in your soul so that you come to have the mind of Christ.*

Guidance with the Eye

I will instruct you and teach you in the way you should go;
I will guide you with My eye.

PSALM 32:8 NKJV

We are guided by others' eyes in two ways. First, very few children, wives or husbands have not been forcibly guided by the stare of their parent or partner! But we're also guided by another's eye when we work or play closely with another—as on a team. We sense their intentions and thoughts because we're aware of what they are focused upon. That's why people who work together effectively don't have to be told what the other is thinking or what they should do to help. Model employees are not those who wait for someone to tell them what to do. Everyone breathes more easily when the new person on the job no longer has to be told what to do at every stage.

In the same way, we are guided by God's "eye" when our will and thoughts are immersed in what God is doing in this world and the attitudes in which God customarily works.

PRAY: *Pray about what God is doing in this world that you are or want to be part of. Say back to God what you think his thoughts are about this endeavor. Tell God you wish to know more of his mind on this matter.*

MONDAY

Inhabited Ones

> *In him the whole building is joined together and rises*
> *to become a holy temple in the Lord.*
> *And in him you too are being built together to become a dwelling*
> *in which God lives by his Spirit.*
>
> EPHESIANS 2:21-22

In *The Transforming Friendship*, Leslie Weatherhead describes a kind of friendship interaction that occurs beyond words:

> [Let's say] my friend's mother in a distant town falls ill and he urgently desires to visit her. Which would reveal deeper friendship [between us]—my lending him my motor-bike in response to his request for it, or my taking it to his door for him as soon as I heard of the need, without waiting to be asked.

In the first case the friend has to ask, but in the second the friendship creates a longing to help. The second illustrates communion at a deeper level, where a friend simply knows the mind of the other. This unspoken level of communication with God occurs as we become the temple of God that understands and cooperates with his purposes and is inhabited through a willing, clear-eyed identification of ourselves with Jesus Christ.

MEDITATE: *Read Ephesians 2:21-22 aloud slowly. Then say aloud, "I am one who is inhabited through a willing, clear-eyed identification with Jesus Christ." Repeat this process. Respond to God in prayer, thanking him for inhabiting you.*

Not Having to Wonder

> *Then Jesus asked them,*
> *"Which is lawful on the Sabbath: to do good or to do evil,*
> *to save life or to kill?" But they remained silent.*

MARK 3:4

In many cases our need to be told what God wants in a certain situation indicates how little we are engaged in his work. When Jesus came upon a man with a withered hand in the synagogue one sabbath, he called him up and asked the people gathered whether one should do good on the sabbath (heal the man) or do evil (leave him in distress). Their silence declared their inner condition. They did not know what to do! After Jesus healed the man, they thought they knew what God wanted: to kill Jesus (Mark 3:1-5)! Jesus knew what God wanted done because he knew the mind of God.

Our union with God involves conversational relationship with God as his friend and colaborer in the affairs of the kingdom. It is Christ in us that is our hope of glory (Colossians 1:27).

MEDITATE: *Read Mark 3:1-5. Consider the synagogue folks (primarily Pharisees) who could not automatically want someone healed (love, compassion), but who could automatically want someone dead (judgment, contempt). What causes religious people to be so disconnected with the heart of God? What heart attitudes must have been missing? Plead for them.*

Cooperation, Not Dictation

> *Therefore, my dear friends, as you have always obeyed—not only in my presence,*
> *but now much more in my absence—continue to work out your salvation with*
> *fear and trembling, for it is God who works in you to will and*
> *to act according to his good purpose.*

PHILIPPIANS 2:12-13

In the *message-a-minute view* of hearing God, God is either telling you what to do at every turn of the road or would tell you if you'd only ask. But Peter and Paul (according to our evidence) were not constantly receiving communications from God. Nor was Jesus. The union Christ had with the Father was the greatest that we can conceive of in this life, yet we have no indication that Jesus was constantly awash with revelations about what he should do. His union with the Father was so great that he was at all times obedient. Yet this obedience rested in his mature will and understanding of his life before God, not on always being told "Now do this" about every detail of life. Even though God works through the Holy Spirit and the indwelling Christ to speak to us, God does not keep us constantly under his dictation.

REFLECT: *What notions of insecurity cause people to want God to direct their lives every minute? What does it say about God that he prefers to work in us?*

Hooked on Miracles

When Herod saw Jesus, he was greatly pleased,
because for a long time he had been wanting to see him.
From what he had heard about him, he hoped to see him perform some miracle.

LUKE 23:8

God could deliver a thousand messages or miracles a nanosecond if that would suit his purpose of bringing forth the cosmic family of God. But it does not. Too much intrusion on a seed that has been planted makes normal, healthy growth impossible. Thus, in *A Song of Assents,* E. Stanley Jones helpfully observes,

> I believe in miracle, but not too much miracle, for too much miracle would weaken us, make us dependent on miracle instead of our obedience. Just enough miracle to let us know God is there, but not too much, lest we depend on it when we should depend on our own initiative and on His orderly processes for our development.

Sometimes we get caught up in trying to glorify God by praising what he can do, and we lose sight of the practical point of what he actually does do.

REFLECT: *Consider how God has helped you grow. What seem to be God's favorite methods in drawing you toward him and his kingdom? Miracles? Examining mistakes and making confession? Teaching and study? Learning from others' examples? Serving alongside others? Is there one of these you need to allow God to use more fully?*

Bible Roulette

> *My sheep listen to my voice;*
> *I know them, and they follow me.*
>
> JOHN 10:27

People tell of opening the Bible at random, stabbing their finger on the page and reading the selected verse to decide whether to move or undertake some enterprise. While this Bible roulette method intends to honor the Bible, this zeal is not based on knowledge (Romans 10:2).

Of course, God is so great that he sometimes uses anything you can imagine for his purposes in the life of a person who is sincerely seeking him. Even truly superstitious methods are not beyond God's use. But that does not certify them as methods chosen by him for the spiritual life.

Many who act upon such "guidance" do great harm to themselves and others around them. What a stark contrast to losers at Bible roulette are those who hear Christ's voice and Christ knows them and they follow him. Their aloneness is banished and the meaning and full purpose of human existence is realized.

PRAY: *Speak to God about your view of him. Do you see God as one who keeps you dangling, playing guessing games? How convinced are you that God's presence is so actual that your aloneness is banished? That God gives meaning and full purpose to your existence? Thank God for the light you have. Request more light as needed.*

Believing Whatever Comes

Ask and it will be given to you; seek and you will find;
knock and the door will be opened to you.

MATTHEW 7:7

People sometimes say, "Whatever comes is God's will" or "Everything happens for a reason." Although this view brings peace of mind, it is flawed. Many things that happen are not God's will, even though God does not stop them. For example, "the Lord is . . . not wanting anyone to perish, but everyone to come to repentance" (2 Peter 3:9), but countless people don't repent. Just because something happens doesn't indicate that it's God's will. Besides, what happens is never just a matter of *whatever* comes. You contributed to it in some way. Not everything you choose to do is God's will.

We have an indispensable role to play in God's world. The issue is not simply what God wants but also what we want. Regarding many things, God's will is that we should determine what will happen. What a child does when not told what to do is the final indicator of what and who that child is. And so it is for us and our heavenly Father.

REFLECT: *Have you been passively accepting whatever happens as God's will? Have you lacked confidence in God or lacked initiative in asking him for what you believe to be good or for understanding about how he wants to involve you?*

M O N D A Y *A Voice in the Dark*

> *Love the LORD your God, listen to his voice, and hold fast to him.*
> *For the LORD is your life, and he will give you many years in the land he*
> *swore to give to your fathers, Abraham, Isaac and Jacob.*

DEUTERONOMY 30:20

In Britain on a foggy, pitch-black night, Peter Marshall, a widely acclaimed minister of the past, was taking a shortcut across the moors. As he plodded blindly forward, an urgent voice called out, "Peter!" He stopped and answered: "Yes, who is it? What do you want?" But there was no response. Thinking he was mistaken, he took a few more steps. The voice came again, more urgently: "Peter!" He stopped again and, trying to peer into the darkness, stumbled forward and fell to his knees. Putting down his hand to brace himself, he found nothing there. As he felt around he discovered that he was right on the brink of an abandoned limestone quarry, where one step more would have killed him.

Such stories as this one, recorded by Catherine Marshall in *A Man Called Peter,* serve as an essential point of reference for research into listening to God's voice.

MEDITATE: *Read Deuteronomy 30:20 and notice the three commands in the first sentence. Ponder their order and progression. How does the Lord actually become the "life" of one who behaves in such a way? Respond to God in prayer.*

Preexisting Ideas

> *Jesus replied, "You are in error because you do not know*
> *the Scriptures or the power of God."*

MATTHEW 22:29

If we are limited by our preexisting ideas and assumptions, no amount of stories, signs or miraculous events will convince us that God will speak to us. These ideas determine what we can see or hear and how we interpret Scripture and others' stories about hearing God.

In Jesus' account of the rich man and Lazarus, the rich man wanted father Abraham to "send Lazarus to my father's house" to convince them to be kind and avoid this "place of torment" (Luke 16:27, 28). Abraham wisely replied that if the rich man's brothers on earth "do not listen to Moses and the prophets they will pay no heed even if someone should rise from the dead" (v. 31). Their preexisting ideas defeated them.

Warning them would have been fruitless against their false preexisting ideas. Their limited understanding of Scripture and of the power of God kept them from genuine faith in him.

REFLECT: *What possible preexisting ideas keep you from hearing God? Notions that you aren't important to God? That God doesn't want to relate to us? What, if anything, might hold you back?*

God Speaking to Us Through Us

> *Jesus replied, "Blessed are you, Simon son of Jonah, for this was not revealed to you by man, but by my Father in heaven."*

MATTHEW 16:17

God is always trying to teach us about himself. In my experience the illuminating word given *to* me by God is often spoken *by* me. It comes out with no preliminaries. I've come to recognize it, but I do not always understand its true significance at the time.

Peter's great confession is an example of this: "You are the Messiah, the Son of the living God" (Matthew 16:16 NRSV). Jesus authenticated that this word given to Peter was indeed from the Father (v. 17). Then he explained further what was going to happen to him—persecution, death, resurrection. Immediately Peter showed that he did not understand what he himself had just said. God had enabled Peter to recognize Jesus as the Christ, but Peter still did not know that "the Christ" would not be a strictly human role (vv. 18-23). Like Peter, we may need time to understand what God has said *to* us *through* us.

REFLECT: *Under what circumstances are you most likely to say or think something insightful that astounds you? For example, it might happen during a powerful teaching session, while talking with a certain friend or in distracting moments doing yard work or another task.*

God's Lowliness

> *Let the little children come to me, and do not hinder them,*
> *for the kingdom of heaven belongs to such as these.*

MATTHEW 19:14

But isn't God too great to engage run-of-the-mill human beings in conversation? This is to confuse God's greatness with human greatness, which we think involves snobbishness and avoiding ordinary people. If great humans don't associate with ordinary people, God certainly wouldn't talk to *us*. God is like a busy dignitary, too conscious of his status to bother with average people.

How hard it is for us to come to an adequate conception of the *lowliness* of God! His greatness is precisely what makes him ready to hear and speak personally with his creatures. Jesus' actions and words made clear how accessible God is to the weak and downtrodden, even children. One characteristic of children is their relative unimportance, but the humanly unimportant ones are important to God. God being who God is, and revealed in the person of Jesus Christ, we should be surprised if he does *not* speak to us.

PRAY: *Respond to God regarding his lowliness. You might thank God for loving and speaking to ordinary human beings (such as Abraham, David and Mary). Ask God to give you a greater sense of his exhaustive nature to encompass such lowliness with such greatness.*

Ears to Hear

> *If anyone has ears to hear, let him hear.*
> *Consider carefully what you hear. . . . With the measure you use,*
> *it will be measured to you—and even more.*

MARK 4:23-24

People who don't hear God insist he doesn't speak to them, but perhaps their hearing is not "in tune." Radio and television messages pass through our bodies and brains all day, but we aren't appropriately tuned receivers so we can't pluck them from the air. In the same way, we are showered with God's messages, but they go past us because we are not *attuned* to God's voice.

Some of Jesus' deepest teachings are about hearing. He taught in parables so those who did not really want to hear the truth could avoid it. He explained that not everyone has ears for the straightforward purpose of hearing, so they use their ears to sift out what they don't want to hear. He urged his hearers to make a great effort to hear, assuring them that the measure they received would be proportional to the measure of their desire and effort.

REFLECT: *Consider to what "measure" you are willing to hear God. What sorts of things would a person do who was immeasurably willing to hear God? What would his or her life be like? How different would it be from yours today?*

Ready Vessels

Search me, O God, and know my heart; test me and know my anxious thoughts.
See if there is any offensive way in me, and lead me in the way everlasting.

P S A L M   1 3 9 : 2 3 - 2 4

Even though God speaks to many people, some do not hear because they are not ready vessels. People are unprepared vessels when *they can't make good use of a word from God because of how they are living.* So we ask ourselves: *Do I stand ready to obey and change, should God direct that? Do I want to know if I am wrong? To what use would I try to put a word from God?* This requires honest soul-searching.

Hearing God—as a reliable, day-to-day reality—is for the disciple of Jesus Christ who has no higher preference than to be like him.

PRAY: *Pray Psalm 139:23-24 and search yourself in God's presence. Do you stand ready to obey and change, should that be what God directs? Where are you most resistant to hearing God's direction (for example, in circumstances that require humility or honesty or purity)? Do you want to know if you are on a wrong path? When you sit down to read or hear a sermon, are you willing to ask God to show you where you are wrong and what you need to know to be corrected?*

M O N D A Y *Guidance as a Gimmick*

> *So they asked him, "What miraculous sign then will you give*
> *that we may see it and believe you? What will you do? . . .*
> *From now on give us this bread."*

JOHN 6:30, 34

People are unprepared vessels when *they unconsciously wish to use* God's guidance as a gimmick for gain. We cannot call on God for help to perform for us—to beat our competitors, to win bets on football matches or to prove that we are theologically correct. While guidance is available to every person who walks with God, it is not *at our disposal as we see fit.* How different is the simple request, "Give us this day our daily bread," from the crowd's demand: "Sir, from now on give us this bread" (Matthew 6:11; John 6:34).

We must always consider the purposes of God: "Hallowed be *Thy* name. *Thy* kingdom come. *Thy* will be done." All God's activities in us serve these purposes. Those who are living day to day as the friends of Christ are devoted to the glory of God and the advancement of his kingdom.

PRAY: *Read the verses above and grieve over those who use God, the gospel and God's guidance for personal gain. Ask that they might come to be true friends of Christ who are devoted to the glory of God. Close by praying the Lord's Prayer, emphasizing* Thy *as shown above.*

Living for One Thing

For to me, to live is Christ and to die is gain.

PHILIPPIANS 1:21

If you believe God has never spoken to you, ask yourself what you are doing that would give God reason to speak to you. Are you and God in business together in life, or are you in business for yourself, trying to "use a little God" to advance your projects?

When our lives are devoted to the will of God, he has reason to speak to us. If our lives aren't devoted to his purposes, he still may use us for his ends if we are strategically placed. We are his creatures no matter how misguided or rebellious.

We are more likely to hear God when we can say, "I am living for one thing and one thing only—to be like Christ, to do his work and serve his people and him. My life is to bless others in the name of God."

MEDITATE: *Read Philippians 1:21 aloud and ask, "Am I using God to fix my world or am I immersing myself in God's great world and learning to live my life the way Christ would if he were me?" Turn your answer into a prayer that might begin "Yes, I am . . . " or "I would like to . . ." or "Please help me . . ."*

God's Word Can Disturb Us

For this is what you asked of the LORD your God at Horeb on the day of the assembly
when you said, "Let us not hear the voice of the LORD our God nor
see this great fire anymore, or we will die."

DEUTERONOMY 18:16

Perhaps we do not hear the voice of God because we know subconsciously that we intend to run our lives on our own. The voice of God would therefore be an unwelcome intrusion into our plans. His word might be a disturbing element into our lives, just as the Israelites believed that to hear the voice of God would bring death.

In *How to Live*, G. Campbell Morgan addresses the person who makes his own plans and lives where he pleases, never hearing God's disturbing voice: "You know no disturbing voice? God never points out for you a pathway altogether different from the one you had planned? Then, my brother, you are living still in the land of slavery, in the land of darkness."

In truth, when we welcome God's voice, we find ourselves enveloped in God's loving companionship.

REFLECT: *In what areas of life do you wish that God would not disturb you by talking about it to you? Where do you wish God would leave well enough alone? How would your character have to change to welcome God's words in that area of life?*

Nature: Hindrance or Help?

For what can be known about God is plain to them,
because God has shown it to them.
Ever since the creation of the world his eternal power and divine nature,
invisible though they are, have been understood and seen through the things he has made.

ROMANS 1:19-20 NRSV

Hearing God seems impossible to some because of the brutal ravages of war, disasters and illness. Even nature seems to run with no assistance from God. We cry out, but the word of God does not seem to come and we are not at peace.

Even in those moments, the evidence of God is obvious to the earnest seeker. God's fingerprints are all over the purposeful order of nature, history and our individual lives. The apostle Paul had this in mind when he said that God has so arranged our world that we should seek the Lord and "by feeling [our] way toward him, succeed in finding him. Yet in fact he is not far from any of us, since it is in him that we live, and move, and exist" (Acts 17:27-28 JB).

PRAY: *Read Romans 1:19-20 outdoors. Pray these verses back to God: "O God, you are plain to me in . . . Your power and divine nature are evident to me in . . ." As you pray, hold a natural object in your hands and ponder it.*

Hearing God Is Not "Scientific"

> The earth is the LORD's, and everything in it,
> the world, and all who live in it.
>
> PSALM 24:1

Science and theology seem to have been at war in Western civilization for the last several hundred years. Scientific knowledge is assumed to exclude the presence of God from the material universe, in which we human beings supposedly play a small and insignificant part. It now seems unscientific to speak of hearing God. Because science is a weighty authority in our lives, we have difficulty hearing God if we believe it is unscientific.

Hearing God is not, however, unscientific when you understand that *the whole of reality is penetrated through and through by God.* Then you can open yourself up to receiving a direct communication from him. Heaven really is right here. Over and over, God spoke to Abraham, Hagar, Jacob, Moses and so on "out of heaven" or "from heaven," which was right beside them. The kingdom of God is among us—a dynamic, unseen system of divine reality in which we move about.

REFLECT: *Review your research as a spiritual scientist. What have you learned through trial and error (AKA experiments) about hearing from God through prayer (AKA intimate research on having a relationship with God)? What works for you in prayer that you've never read in a book? (Scientists come up with original findings.)*

Mind over Matter

For by him all things were created: things in heaven and on earth, visible and invisible,
whether thrones or powers or rulers or authorities; all things were created by him and for him.
He is before all things, and in him all things hold together.

COLOSSIANS 1:16-17

In previous centuries the physical sciences viewed the universe as machine-like, operating in crudely mechanical ways. Current views are more congenial to God's presence in the world. In *The Mysterious Universe,* Sir James Jean interpreted the result of twentieth-century developments in physics as follows:

> Today the stream of knowledge is heading towards a non-mechanical reality; the universe begins to look more like a *great thought* than like a great machine. *Mind* no longer appears as an accidental intruder into the realm of matter; we are beginning to suspect that we ought rather to hail it as the *creator* and *governor* of the realm of matter. (emphasis added)

The New Testament presents Christ as the glue of the universe. "In him all things hold together" (Colossians 1:17). Since it is the nature of mind, always and everywhere, to guide, is it not therefore reasonable to *expect* guidance and communication from God?

M E D I T A T E : *Read Colossians 1:16-17 and ponder Christ as the "mind" that is the "creator and governor of the realm of matter." Praise Christ in God for being the master of molecules.*

Spring

M O N D A Y

No Telephone Lines Needed

He is not far from each one of us.
"For in him we live and move and have our being."
As some of your own poets have said, "We are his offspring."

ACTS 17:27-28

Ordinarily we must make use of some kind of connecting device to communicate across a distance. To make a long-distance telephone call, one must use telephone lines so that electrical impulses are received halfway around the world into a form that a faraway friend can hear. Even if I wish to speak directly to you as you stand next to me, I must make noise with my vocal cords that strikes your eardrums, which causes you to think of specific things or events.

What surprises us is that God does *not* need connecting devices to communicate with us (although at times he chooses to use Scripture or other people). God has placed us in a material world that permits him to be near to us—even nearer than our own eyes, ears and brain. How do we live and move and have our being? "In him" (Acts 17:28).

REFLECT: *What does it mean to you to be in God? Have you spiritualized that away to mean some future position in heaven and not a here-and-now way of existing? How would a conscious reality of always being in God make you better able to hear him?*

Then Elisha prayed: "O LORD, please open his eyes that he may see."
So the LORD opened the eyes of the servant, and he saw;
the mountain was full of horses and chariots of fire all around Elisha.

2 KINGS 6:17 NRSV

We need to have our understanding changed the way Elisha's young assistant's was. The king of Syria decided to "get Elisha" because Elisha kept miraculously revealing this king's battle plans to the king of Israel (2 Kings 6:12). When Elisha's young helper stepped outside one morning, he found they were completely surrounded by Syrian troops and he was terrified. "Don't be afraid," the prophet told him. "Those who are with us are more than those who are with them." Elisha prayed, and the assistant saw the chariots of fire protecting them (2 Kings 6:16-17).

God enabled the young man to see the powers of his realm that totally interpenetrated and upheld the visible reality around him. How we need Elishas today who, by life and teaching and prayer, might open our eyes to see the reality of God's presence all around us.

P R A Y : *Consider a situation in your life that seems overwhelming. Then pray Elisha's prayer for yourself. Allow God to show you details of the situation or "chariots of fire" surrounding you. Or pray his prayer for someone who is assisting you as Elisha did for his assistant.*

Surprised by God

> When Jacob awoke from his sleep, he thought,
> "Surely the LORD is in this place, and I was not aware of it."
> He was afraid and said, "How awesome is this place!
> This is none other than the house of God; this is the gate of heaven."

GENESIS 28:16-17

In our "existence as usual" we are like Jacob in sorrow, alienation and loneliness, asleep in a desert ravine. But in his dream—or was he only then truly awake?—he saw God interacting where he lay. "He saw a stairway resting on the earth, with its top reaching to heaven, and the angels of God were ascending and descending on it" (Genesis 28:12). God said, "All peoples on earth will be blessed through you and your offspring. I am with you and will watch over you wherever you go, and I will bring you back to this land. I will not leave you until I have done what I have promised you" (vv. 14-15).

Awakening, Jacob cried out that God had been there after all. Jacob's entire perspective was changed. There is no place where God is not, and we will know this as we learn to pay attention.

REFLECT: *In what ordinary places do you expect the sustaining word of God to be? In what "existence as usual" places would you be surprised to have God speak to you?*

The Church of "Living Stones"

> *Would that all the LORD's people were prophets,*
> *and that the LORD would put his spirit on them!*
>
> NUMBERS 11:29 NRSV

In humility and generosity of great heart, Moses cried the above. But would it really work for all God's people to be prophets? If individual believers lived in a conversational relationship with God, wouldn't that lead to chaos in the church? Wouldn't people contradict and criticize one another based on their private "conversations" with God? Yet to keep this from happening would require a hierarchy of authority and subordination, in which one person speaks for God and thus enforces conformity in the church.

The core issue is the model of leadership and authority that is suitable for the redeemed community, which is living out the good news of God's reign in the context of human life. "Living stones" (1 Peter 2:5) in conversation with God himself begin to look much better, despite all their problems, once we compare them to the alternative—dead stones.

PRAY: *Pray for yourself as a "living stone" to be "built into a spiritual house to be a holy priesthood" that you would "offer spiritual sacrifices acceptable to God through Jesus Christ" (1 Peter 2:5). Then pray this for followers of Jesus you know who are eager to know and hear God.*

FRIDAY *Sheepdogs or Shepherds?*

But I, when I am lifted up from the earth,
will draw all men to myself.

JOHN 12:32

To *lead* people is not to manipulate, drive or manage them. The sheepdog forcibly maneuvers the sheep, whereas the biblical shepherd calls as he calmly walks ahead of the sheep. This distinction between the sheepdog and the shepherd is profoundly significant as we lead Christ's people—and through our influence we all lead others, whether it be groups or friends or children. As leaders, we must frequently ask ourselves which role we are fulfilling.

When we lead as shepherds, our confidence is in only the word of the Great Shepherd coming to his sheep through us or otherwise. When they know his voice, they will not follow another (John 10:1-16). We do not *want* them to follow another, even if we are that "other." God draws people (John 12:32) and uproots people (Matthew 15:13), while our job is to lift up Christ who said: "All that the Father gives me will come to me, and whoever comes to me I will never drive away" (John 6:37).

PRAY: *Think about a situation or person you are tempted to "forcibly maneuver" in some way. Pray that God will do the drawing or uprooting. Ask God to show you how to be a shepherd in this situation or this person's life instead of a sheepdog.*

Relying on God's Strength

If anyone speaks, he should do it as one speaking the very words of God.
If anyone serves, he should do it with the strength God provides,
so that in all things God may be praised through Jesus Christ.

1 PETER 4:11

Servants of God count on those to whom they minister to also minister to them. Ministry is never a one-way street when it is functioning rightly in any group. As Henri Nouwen wrote in *Creative Ministry,* "A redemptive teaching relationship is bilateral. . . . The teacher has to learn from his student. . . . Teachers and students are fellowmen who together are searching for what is true, meaningful, and valid, and who give each other the chance to play each other's roles."

A shepherd never stoops to drive, manipulate or manage people, relying only on human abilities and powers inherent in unassisted human nature, instead of serving or speaking with "the strength God provides" (1 Peter 4:11).

PRAY: *Pray for someone you are currently helping—perhaps with doing chores or teaching or welcoming into a group. Ask God to continue giving you strength in this. Also ask God to show you how this person(s) is now ministering to you in ways you have not seen.*

MONDAY *Servant Leadership*

> Be shepherds of God's flock that is under your care,
> serving as overseers—not because you must, but because you are willing,
> as God wants you to be; not greedy for money, but eager to serve;
> not lording it over those entrusted to you, but being examples to the flock.

1 PETER 5:2-3

With those we lead in any way (sometimes we lead by simply asking the right questions), we are to be "the servant of all" (Mark 9:35), "eager to serve; not lording it over those entrusted to you" (1 Peter 5:2-3). Redemptive mutual submission (Ephesians 5:21) is achieved in this way.

So much current religious work is not lined up with these scriptural injunctions. This is bound to be if those who lead try to control the flock through their own abilities to organize and drive, yet clothed in a spiritual terminology. They do not rely on Christ's power. As their faith is, so shall their leadership be. It will be "my group," "my ministry" and "my children"—and those who follow will never experience how completely *God* is Lord of each person.

REFLECT: *Ponder the phrase "redemptive mutual submission." How does God want you to be redemptive in others' lives—pointing them to Christ and assisting them in becoming Christlike? How does God want you to be mutually submissive in your relationships—not trying to control others but "eager to serve"?*

TUESDAY

Leadership: Cultic or Christlike?

Test everything. Hold on to the good.

1 THESSALONIANS 5:21

Most of the cults active in the United States are based on the premise that God speaks to one or several central people in the group in a way that he does not speak to the ordinary members. These members are taught not to trust their own minds or their own communications with God except within the context of the group, with all its pressures toward conformity to the leaders' words. Frequently adherents are taught to accept pronouncements that are self-contradictory and fly in the face of all common sense if the leader says they must.

Certain models of leadership in the average church, however, also use these methods, especially those that promote "groupthink" and focus on personalities of leaders. As a leader, I must ask *myself* to what extent *I* urge people to conform or to support *my* plans (perhaps unconsciously or in hopes of helping people get along), so that people put away their minds and their own individual experiences of guidance and communication with their Lord.

PRAY: *Ask God to help those seeking God around you to "test everything" and "hold on to the good." Specifically ask that they would grow wise in hearing God, learn to use their minds, trust their communications with God and examine if what they believe he is saying to them is self-contradictory.*

> *Do nothing out of selfish ambition or vain conceit,*
> *but in humility consider others better than yourselves.*

PHILIPPIANS 2:3

Everyone personally conferring with God does risk disagreements and un-cooperativeness. Leaders may find themselves questioned and examined—perhaps overturned—by those they are appointed to lead. If leaders are to succeed in leading, they will need the safeguard of others' discernment as well as a genuine authority from the Lord. They will also need a true humility—everyone thinking others better than themselves—for them to carry on with their work.

Of course there *is* a subordination within the fellowship of believers, but it does not come from struggling for authority. Rather authority comes from experience in the Way and by speaking what is truly God's word. Then the true unity and power of the glorious body of Christ will be fully realized. This unity is the light of the world, the end and aim of all human history.

REFLECT: *Consider how open you are to the Spirit of God speaking through those who question you. Can you stand to be earnestly questioned without taking it personally? Are you willing to have your ideas overturned in an honest search for truth? As you listen to a sermon or read a book, do you routinely believe that the speaker or author can teach you and that you need to listen diligently?*

Let the word of Christ dwell in you richly as you teach and admonish
one another with all wisdom, and as you sing psalms, hymns and spiritual songs
with gratitude in your hearts to God.

COLOSSIANS 3:16

In matters of hearing God, which is more important: the individual's communion with God or the guidance of the community of Christ? Both. St. Francis de Sales offered practical advice to his student Philothea. In his *Introduction to the Devout Life,* describing "those interior attractions, motions, reproaches and remorses, lights and conceptions which God excites in us" as "inspirations," he directs her, "Resolve, then, Philothea, to accept with a ready heart all the inspirations it shall please God to send to you. Attend calmly to His proposals, think of the love with which you are inspired, and cherish the holy inspiration."

Then St. Francis wisely directs Philothea to the church's fellowship, saying, "But before you consent to inspiration in things which are of great importance, or that are out of the ordinary way, always consult your advisor."

REFLECT: *Notice these imperative verbs directed to Philothea in the quotation by Francis de Sales: accept, attend, think of, cherish, consult. How do you need to respond to God's words to you by cherishing them? By consulting others in Christ's community about them?*

F R I D A Y *Testing Every Spirit*

> *Dear friends, do not believe every spirit,*
> *but test the spirits to see whether they are from God,*
> *because many false prophets have gone out into the world.*

1 J O H N 4 : 1

In *Listening to God,* Joyce Huggett passes on this advice about hearing God: "If you believe God has told you to do something, ask him to confirm it to you three times: through his word, through circumstances, and through other people who may know nothing of the situation." This precept of three witnesses is a good rule of thumb in an area where rules of thumb are badly needed.

We use our good sense in hearing God, but we also ask others to use their good sense for our good. No man or woman is an island, though we are much more than the sum of our relationships to others. They must rest on our personal relationship to God himself. When *both* relationships are right, we find perfect safety and full and perfect peace.

REFLECT: *How do you commonly "test every spirit," or do you just do the "smart" thing or call a few friends and do whatever they advise? Be brutally honest. Ask God to show you what you would do if you chose to "test every spirit" more diligently?*

Earnestly Seeking

*You will seek me and find me
when you seek me with all your heart.*

JEREMIAH 29:13

God does not compete for our attention. In most cases God does *not* run over us, although occasionally he has knocked someone like Saul to the ground. We must be open to God's addressing us in any way he chooses, or else we might walk past a burning bush instead of saying, as Moses did, "I will go over and see this strange sight—why the bush does not burn up" (Exodus 3:3). We may even mistake the voice of God for just another one of our own thoughts.

On the other hand, the reality of God's voice does not make it unnecessary for us to seek it. To seek for something is to look for it everywhere. It is when we *seek* God earnestly, prepared to go out of our way to examine anything that might be his overture toward us—including the most obvious things like Bible verses or our own thoughts—that he promises to be found (Jeremiah 29:13).

PRAY: *Ask God to help you seek him more earnestly, to go out of your way to examine anything that might be him approaching you. Perhaps you need to acknowledge that you've expected him to compete for your attention or knock you over the head.*

MONDAY *Wonders Never Cease*

The word of the LORD came to Abram in a vision:
"Do not be afraid, Abram. I am your shield, your very great reward." . . .
When the sun had set and darkness had fallen, a smoking firepot
with a blazing torch appeared and passed between the pieces [of the sacrifices].

GENESIS 15:1, 17

One way in which people are addressed by God within the biblical record is with a *phenomenon plus a voice.* A phenomenon is an occurrence that can be perceived by any of our senses. For example, it might be an appearance of something unusual. God often accompanies such phenomena with a voice. Such divine-human encounters are richly represented in the events of Scripture, and we need to use our imagination to identify with them.

God's covenant with Abram, a major foundation of the Judeo-Christian tradition, was solemnized when fire from God passed through the air to consume Abram's sacrifice while God intoned the promise to Abram and his seed (Genesis 15:17-18).

MEDITATE: *Read Genesis 15:1-17. Notice Abram's questions within the conversation between God and him (vv. 1-9). Now imagine Abram preparing sacrifices and desperately driving away the predatory birds from them. See the setting sun and the dreadful darkness as Abram falls into a deep sleep. Once again God speaks to Abram and the torch-laden firepot lights the sacrifices. Reread the passage and sit quietly basking in Abram's experiences.*

Unusual Appearances

When you heard the voice out of the darkness,
while the mountain was ablaze with fire,
all the leading men of your tribes and your elders came to me.
And you said, "The LORD our God has shown us his glory and his majesty,
and we have heard his voice from the fire. Today we have seen that
a man can live even if God speaks with him."

D E U T E R O N O M Y   5 : 2 3 - 2 4

Scripture records several accounts of God addressing people with a phenomenon accompanied by a voice. Besides Moses receiving his call as God spoke from a burning bush (Exodus 3:3-6), the nation of Israel was called to covenant by God's voice from within a mountain on fire, pulsating with presence (Deuteronomy 5:23). Ezekiel was addressed in the context of a meteorological display that defies all but poetic description (Ezekiel 1—2).

At Jesus' baptism the Spirit visibly descended upon him as a voice from heaven spoke (Matthew 3:16-17). Saul's encounter with Christ on the road to Damascus involved a blinding light from heaven and an audible voice (Acts 9:3-8). Such events reveal God's method of speaking through a phenomenon accompanied by a voice.

M E D I T A T E : *Picture yourself as an Israelite experiencing the events described in Deuteronomy 5:23-24. What would you have seen and heard and smelled and felt in the air? Say verse 24 aloud. Consider that something like this might happen to you, should God choose it.*

Reacting to Experiences

We have not stopped praying for you and asking God to fill you with
the knowledge of his will through all spiritual wisdom and understanding . . .
giving thanks to the Father, who has qualified you to share in the
inheritance of the saints in the kingdom of light.

COLOSSIANS 1:9, 12

When people tell stories of seeing Jesus immersed in light, listeners may discount these stories because "Satan himself masquerades as an angel of light" (2 Corinthians 11:14). Although we cannot dismiss this concern, we must also remember that light *can* serve as Satan's disguise because God *is* light (1 John 1:5), because we are children of light (Ephesians 5:8) and because God makes "his messengers a flaming fire" (Psalm 104:4 KJV). It would be strange to shun what is genuine simply because it resembles what is counterfeit.

Or listeners may consider persons with such experiences to be favored by God and place them above others. They confuse the medium with the message and may worship the experience rather than the One who was supposedly present through it. These people often feel spiritually inferior unless something similar happens to them.

PRAY: *If you know anyone who has had such experiences (including yourself), pray for that person using ideas from Colossians 1:9, 12. If not, pray for those who are now having such experiences, though you may not be aware of it.*

> *The LORD appeared to Abraham near the great trees of Mamre*
> *while he was sitting at the entrance to his tent in the heat of the day.*
> *Abraham looked up and saw three men standing nearby. When he saw them,*
> *he hurried from the entrance of his tent to meet them and bowed low to the ground.*

GENESIS 18:1-2

God also addresses people through supernatural messengers or angels, though they do not always reveal their identity. These supernatural beings move about on divine missions. Sometimes in the biblical record it is difficult to determine whether an angel or the Lord himself is on the scene. For example, the text of Genesis 18 shifts among calling the strangers "they," "the men" and "the LORD." In Genesis 19:1 only two angels appear to Lot in Sodom to finish off the episode. The three men of Genesis 18 were apparently two angels accompanied by the Lord. We never know when we'll be asked to be hospitable to angels (Hebrews 13:2).

M E D I T A T E : *Read Genesis 18:1-33. Notice the ordinary way Abraham sat at his front door in midday—not the mysterious twilight we might expect. The Lord and the angels took the ordinary guise of three strangers needing shelter in this isolated land. Shut your eyes and picture these events. What explanation can you offer for God's choice to appear in such an ordinary way?*

F R I D A Y *A Strategic Meeting*

Now when Joshua was near Jericho, he looked up
and saw a man standing in front of him with a drawn sword in his hand.
Joshua went up to him and asked, "Are you for us or for our enemies?"

JOSHUA 5:13

In front of the city of Jericho, Joshua encounters the "commander of the army of the LORD," who has come to help (Joshua 5:13-15). The commander directs Joshua to take off his shoes because the ground he stands on is holy. The "army of the LORD" here consists mainly of angels, no doubt the same as the legions that became visible to Elisha and his assistant and that later stood at the beck and call of our incarnate Lord (2 Kings 6:17; Matthew 26:53).

A few verses later, the commander now seems to be the Lord himself, explaining that famous and unorthodox military strategy whereby the walls of Jericho were to be brought down with marching, blasting trumpets and shouting (Joshua 6:1-5).

P R A Y : *Think of someone who is fighting a battle of any sort—legal, spiritual, physical, emotional, intellectual. Ask God to stand by that person in a special way, offering ideas for breakthrough. If you think an outward sign would encourage that person, ask for that to occur.*

God Reaching Out

Do not forget to entertain strangers,
for by so doing some people have entertained angels without knowing it.

HEBREWS 13:2

The Bible is a book full of angels, from Genesis 16:7 onward. Human beings are commonly addressed by angels such as in these outstanding cases: Balaam, Gideon, the parents of Samson, Isaiah, Daniel, Joseph, Zacharias, Mary, the women at the empty tomb, Peter and Paul. These people encountered angels in an otherwise normal state of mind, not in dreams and visions. Often, however, the people involved didn't realize they were interacting with an angel of the Lord until the conversation was nearly over (for example, Judges 6:20-22; 13:19-21). How they must have then reflected that the things that occurred were more than a little strange!

REFLECT: *What does it tell you about God that he sends angels to men and women, young and old, apostles and a rogue prophet, a farmer and a politician while they are traveling, working, praying, serving at an altar and even sitting in jail?*

M O N D A Y *Dreaming and Doing*

> *During the night Paul had a vision of a man of Macedonia*
> *standing and begging him, "Come over to Macedonia and help us."*
> *After Paul had seen the vision, we got ready at once to leave for Macedonia,*
> *concluding that God had called us to preach the gospel to them.*

A C T S   1 6 : 9 - 1 0

God may at times address himself to us through dreams and visions. Sometimes they seem to coincide, perhaps because they often come at night and the recipients may not have been able to tell whether they were awake or asleep. So it was with Paul and his vision of the man of Macedonia pleading for help. God spoke to Paul in dreams at other times as well (Acts 18:9; 2 Corinthians 12:1). Both visions and dreams involve a certain detachment from the person's actual surroundings, which marks them off from ordinary waking consciousness.

R E F L E C T : *Perhaps Paul received dreams and visions because God knew he would act on them immediately ("we got ready at once," v. 10), even though he did not hear the message in ordinary waking consciousness. What does Paul's immediacy of obedience in this situation signal about his life with God? Why would God be more likely to speak to such a person in dreams?*

TUESDAY *Discerning Differences*

> *Daniel went in to the king and asked for time,*
> *so that he might interpret the* dream *for him. . . .*
> *During the night the mystery was revealed to Daniel in a vision.*
> *Then Daniel praised the God of heaven and said: "Praise be to the name of God*
> *for ever and ever. . . . He reveals deep and hidden things;*
> *he knows what lies in darkness, and light dwells with him."*

DANIEL 2:16, 19-20, 22 (EMPHASIS ADDED)

Although visions and dreams are similar, they are not always the same. (Daniel knew the difference.) Some visions are not dreams, as with Ananias's vision in which God told him to find Saul, and Peter's rooftop vision of God telling him to eat unclean animals (Acts 9:10-13; 10:9-19). Many dreams are not visions, as with Jacob, Joseph, Joseph's jail mates, Pharaoh and Nebuchadnezzar. Both dreams and visions are unusual states of consciousness, but the dream characteristically requires greater interpretation, often with considerable difficulty.

PRAY: *Ask God for help understanding a recurring dream or recent dream. As you pray, ask God what you need to know about yourself and your world through these dreams you've had. You may wish to paraphrase the words in verse 22: "You, O God, reveal deep and hidden things; you know what lies in darkness, and light dwells with you."*

> *"Let the prophet who has a dream tell his dream,*
> *but let the one who has my word speak it faithfully.*
> *For what has straw to do with grain?" declares the LORD.*
> *"Is not my word like fire," declares the LORD,*
> *"and like a hammer that breaks a rock in pieces?"*

JEREMIAH 23:28-29

By the time of Jeremiah, the understanding of the ways in which God speaks had progressed to the point where the dreaming prophet was treated with some disdain. The dream is considered to be like straw or chaff when compared to the wheat of God's *word* (Jeremiah 23:25-32). God's word is like fire, like a hammer that crushes the rock. The dream has no comparable power.

Gustave Oehler writes in *Theology of the Old Testament* that emerging here is "the principle that a clear consciousness when receiving revelation is placed higher than ecstasy or other abnormal states of mind." This is a vital point to keep in mind as we attempt to understand our *own* experiences of God's communications and the significance of the different ways in which he meets us today.

REFLECT: *Why do you think God seems to value our being clearly conscious when hearing him? What does this tell you about God and our relationship with him? How has the word of God been like wheat to you, feeding your soul?*

The Audible Voice

> But the angel of the LORD called out to him from heaven,
> "Abraham! Abraham!" "Here I am," he replied.
> "Do not lay a hand on the boy," he said. "Do not do anything to him. Now I know that you
> fear God, because you have not withheld from me your son, your only son."

GENESIS 22:11-12

On some occasions God has addressed human beings through what was experienced as an audible voice with nothing else accompanying it. On Mount Moriah, Abraham seems to have heard an audible voice, though involving an angel from heaven, as he was about to sacrifice his son Isaac (Genesis 22:11-12, 15-18).

The cases of God speaking in an audible voice today are often associated with mental unbalance or overactive imagination. While this is no doubt sometimes justified, we must ask ourselves if there are any well-based objections to God's simply producing the sound waves appropriate to audible human language. Skepticism in some cases often rests on outright disbelief in God.

REFLECT: *Consider why people might object to God producing sound waves that resemble human language. Might they unconsciously believe that God is too far away to do this (limiting his omnipresence)? That God cannot duplicate the sound of the human vocal chords (limiting his power)? That God would not lower himself to speak as he's created humans to do? Use these questions to consider the ways we limit God.*

Using the Human Voice

> *Our gospel came to you not simply with words,*
> *but also with power, with the Holy Spirit and with deep conviction.*

1 THESSALONIANS 1:5

The most common means of communication between God and humans in the Bible and history is the voice of an individual human. God and the person he uses speak *conjointly*. The person's words can be both the words of God and their words at the same time. These two activities do not exclude each other any more than humanity and divinity exclude each other in the person of Jesus Christ.

This activity must *not* be understood as a mechanical one, with God simply using the person as a telephone. Samuel Shoemaker has written this excellent description in *With the Holy Spirit and with Fire:*

> We are laid hold of by Something greater than ourselves that expands our energies and capacities. We can accomplish things that in our own strength would have been impossible. . . . The Holy Spirit seems to mix and mingle His power with our own. This is as real and definite as attaching an appliance to an electrical outlet, though of course such a mechanical analogy is not altogether satisfactory.

PRAY: *Thank God for the times the Holy Spirit has mixed and mingled his power with yours. Ask God to help you be cooperative with him, especially in a specific upcoming situation.*

> *But we have this treasure in jars of clay to show that this*
> *all-surpassing power is from God and not from us.*

2 CORINTHIANS 4:7

God's speaking in union with the human voice and human language is the primary way he addresses us from *outside* our own mind or personality. This is well suited to the purposes of God because it *fully engages the faculties of free, intelligent beings who are interacting with agape love in the work of God as his co-laborers and friends.* The accounts in the Bible are full of examples of God enlisting humans as partners in his endeavors. The Bible itself is a case of God speaking along with human beings, first in its delivery to humankind and now as it continues to speak to us today.

It may be that the one spoken *to* is also the one spoken *through*. It is frequently so with me. In this case the word is at once the word of God (God's message) but also the words of the human being who is also speaking.

REFLECT: *Ponder what a person needs to be and do for God to use her or him as a vessel through whom he can speak. What sort of character and inner qualities does such a person need to have?*

M O N D A Y *Help in Speaking*

I will help both of you speak and will teach you what to do.

EXODUS 4:15

When God speaks conjointly with human beings, it often seems he purposely chooses weaker vessels. In Moses' encounter with God through the burning bush, Moses' last line of protest against God's assignment was that he did not speak well: "O Lord, I have never been eloquent, neither in the past nor since you have spoken to your servant. I am slow of speech and tongue" (Exodus 4:10). The Lord's reply was that he, after all, had made human mouths and presumably could assist them to accomplish his assignments: "Now go; I will help you speak and will teach you what to say" (4:12).

When Moses still begged God to send someone else, God angrily gave him Aaron as *his* spokesman. God would speak to Moses, who would speak to Aaron, who would speak to the people. God agreed to speak through both of them (Exodus 4:15), but it seems he would have preferred Moses without Aaron. Speaking well in front of a crowd did not concern God as it did Moses.

PRAY: *Acknowledge to God why and when you are not a polished speaker (perhaps especially when speaking up for truth or offering insights at the appropriate moment). Ask God to use you powerfully in the midst of that weakness.*

TUESDAY
God's Power in My Weakness

> *But he said to me,*
> *"My grace is sufficient for you, for my power is made perfect in weakness."*
> *Therefore I will boast all the more gladly about my weaknesses,*
> *so that Christ's power may rest on me.*

2 CORINTHIANS 12:9

Some New Testament passages suggest that the apostle Paul was not an eloquent speaker. We know from his own statements that, whether by choice or necessity, he did not come among the Corinthians "with eloquence or superior wisdom"; rather he came "in weakness and fear, and with much trembling. My message and my preaching were not with wise and persuasive words, but with a demonstration of the Spirit's power, so that your faith might not rest on men's wisdom, but on God's power" (1 Corinthians 2:1-5). His only confidence was in God speaking *with* him, electrifying his words, as it were, when he spoke.

MEDITATE: *For several moments, sit in the rich phrases of the Scripture quoted above: "[God's] power made perfect in [my] weakness"; "Christ's power may rest on me"; "demonstration of the Spirit and of power." What do such rich phrases cause you to want to pray for yourself? For others you converse with?*

Glorying Only in God

Not many of you were wise by human standards;
not many were influential; not many were of noble birth. . . .
As it is written: "Let him who boasts boast in the Lord."

1 CORINTHIANS 1:26, 31

Those chosen by our Lord to bear his message and carry on his work were frequently "unschooled, ordinary" people (Acts 4:13). In God's selecting them, there would be no mistake about the source of their words and authority.

There must be no misallocation of glory—not because God is a cosmic egotist, but because such a mistake would direct us away from God. It would destroy the blessedness of life in Christ. Hence, the success of the redemptive plan did not require human wisdom or power or status, so that those who gloried would glory only in the Lord (1 Corinthians 1:26, 31).

Moses and Paul, two of the people most responsible for the human authorship of the Bible, were, accordingly, weak with words so that they might have the best chance of clinging constantly to their support in God, who spoke in union with them and so that they might unerringly connect their hearers with God.

PRAY: *Ask the Holy Spirit to help listeners to sermons and readers of books connect directly with God and not be distracted by eloquent or attention-getting speaking and writing.*

Choose for yourselves this day whom you will serve.

JOSHUA 24:15

Does the word of God literally overpower us and compel us to speak? Occasionally those who speak with God seem compelled, such as Balaam. Balak, king of Moab, knew that Balaam spoke in unison with God—"those you bless are blessed, and those you curse are cursed" (Numbers 22:6)—so he offered Balaam great riches and honor if he would curse Israel. Balaam was tempted by the offer and kept toying with the idea. He went along with Balak but found he was *unable* to curse Israel. He explained: "I must speak only what God puts in my mouth" (22:38). Only a stream of blessings came forth (23:7-10).

But this does not mean that the person who speaks in unison with God, and thus speaks the word *of* God, literally cannot help speaking. The individual's compulsion to speak, though often great, is normally still resistible. Human beings are not mere tools or robots.

REFLECT: *Ponder God's enormous respect for the will of a person and God's unwillingness to violate it so that he or she is a "mere tool." People may choose whom they will serve.*

The Power to Speak

> *But as for me, I am filled with power, with the Spirit of the LORD,*
> *and with justice and might, to declare to Jacob his transgression, to Israel his sin.*

MICAH 3:8

Those who understand what it is to speak for and with God are not mere tools, but they find God's word to be of great power, as the prophet Micah exulted in the power he felt surging within him. Jeremiah experienced God's word as a fire that scorches and like a hammer that breaks rocks.

Some may resolve not to speak for the Lord, but like Jeremiah, they find they must: "If I say, 'I will not mention him, or speak any more in his name,' then within me there is something like a burning fire shut up in my bones; I am weary with holding it in, and I cannot" (Jeremiah 20:9 NRSV).

J. B. Phillips said somewhere that, while he was doing his well-known translation of the New Testament, he often felt like an electrician working on the wiring of a house with the power on.

PRAY: *Use Micah 3:8 as a prayer, asking to be "filled with power, with the Spirit of the LORD, and with justice and might." Pray about upcoming conversations and teaching opportunities, that God's power will show itself.*

The Human Spirit

To this end I labor, struggling with all his energy,
which so powerfully works in me.

COLOSSIANS 1:29

Our own human spirit is still another means through which God addresses us. Within our thoughts and feelings, we hear the "still, small voice" of God, an active "energy, which so powerfully works in me." Of the ways in which a message comes from *within* a person (such as dreams and visions), it most commonly comes in the form of their thoughts and feelings—at least for those who are living in harmony with God. Of all these inward routes, this mode is best suited to the redemptive purposes of God because it most engages the faculties of free, intelligent beings involved in the work of God as his colaborers and friends.

One's own spirit can then work together with the Almighty God, using one's thoughts and feelings to bring the truth of his word and his understanding to bear upon one's heart, life and world.

REFLECT: *Think about the idea that God speaks in the form of your thoughts, yet these thoughts are in a sense not yours because they do not originate from you. How do such God-originated thoughts differ from your usual way of thinking? How do these God-originated thoughts reflect God's personality instead?*

MONDAY *The Still, Small Voice*

> *And, behold, the LORD passed by, and a great and strong wind rent the mountains,*
> *and brake in pieces the rocks before the LORD; but the LORD was not in the wind:*
> *and after the wind an earthquake; but the LORD was not in the earthquake:*
> *and after the earthquake a fire; but the LORD was not in the fire:*
> *and after the fire a still small voice.*

1 KINGS 19:11-12 KJV

God addresses us in dreams, visions and voices as well as through the Bible and extraordinary events. Such things are well documented in biblical and personal accounts. The *significance* of these ways can confuse us, however. For example, the still, small voice is so humble that it may be ignored or even discounted by some who think that only the more dramatic communications can be authentic. If this view is accepted, a *life* of hearing God must be filled with constant fireworks from heaven, which is not reasonable. Rather the still, small voice is one of God's primary ways of addressing us.

MEDITATE: *Close your eyes and put yourself in the place of Elijah. Tense up as the strong wind creates havoc. Brace yourself as the ground under your feet keeps shifting. Feel the heat of the fire and see yourself moving away from it. Then perk up to the still, small voice. What does God want to say to you today?*

Talking with a Friend

Whether you turn to the right or to the left,
your ears will hear a voice behind you, saying, "This is the way; walk in it."

ISAIAH 30:21

The still, small voice—or the interior or inner voice, as it is also called—is the preferred and most valuable form of individualized communication for God's purposes. God usually addresses individually those who walk with him in a mature, personal relationship using this inner voice, proclaiming and showing forth the reality of the kingdom of God as they go.

This inner voice is apt communication of God's presence in our lives as a close personal friend, a presence shared by the whole Christian community. It aids in developing our individual personalities into his likeness and in coming to live confidently and sensibly with God as a conversational presence in our lives.

PRAY: *Speak to God about your response to his continually insisting on being your close personal friend. If you wish, offer your amazement that God is not content to be a boss or a distant manager. Consider thanking God for choosing to shape your personality in such a relational way.*

Learning to Recognize the Voice

> *Then Eli realized that the LORD was calling the boy.*
> *So Eli told Samuel, "Go and lie down, and if he calls you, say,*
> *'Speak, LORD, for your servant is listening.'"*

1 SAMUEL 3:8-9

A touching, informative and profound story is that of the child Samuel learning to recognize God's voice, which he experienced as an audible voice. As he slept one night, he heard someone calling his name. He ran to his old master, Eli, thinking Eli had called him. Because God rarely spoke and gave no visions at this time in Israel's history, such things were not discussed. Hence, "Samuel did not yet know the LORD: The word of the LORD had not yet been revealed to him" (3:7).

The third time Samuel thought he'd heard Eli, Eli recognized what was happening. He told Samuel to lie down and answer God's voice. And so it happened. Thus began one of the most remarkable careers of any person who has ever lived before the Lord, fully justifying the use of the phrase "conversational relationship."

MEDITATE: *Read 1 Samuel 3:1-10. If you had been Samuel, how would it have felt to have God speak to you instead of Eli? To have this happen to you when "there were not many visions" (v. 1)? Wrap yourself in the person of young Samuel and feel his wonder at what was happening.*

How precious to me are your thoughts, O God! How vast is the sum of them!

PSALM 139:17

At first the inner voice of God is not always precious to you. You may not be all that conscious of hearing it. Like little Samuel you may not know what this voice is or even that there is such a thing. That is because the still, small voice doesn't always force itself to the front of your thoughts. You don't have to have a theory or doctrine *about* this voice in order to hear it. It is also possible for someone who regularly interacts with the voice of God not to recognize it as something special.

We may not recognize it because those most adept at the divine-human conversation are often reluctant to speak much about the inner voice (in contrast to those who have some of the more spectacular experiences). And that is completely as it should be. God's communication with the individual is precious. It is not for show-and-tell any more than intimate interchanges between two people generally are.

PRAY: *Ask God to train you to cherish his thoughts as they come to you. Perhaps you'd like to practice by moving through a favorite passage of Scripture and saying to God with each phrase: "Thank you for this precious thought. I need it to help me today."*

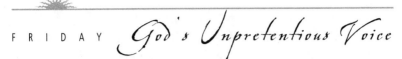
A spirit glided past my face, and the hair on my body stood on end.
It stopped, but I could not tell what it was. A form stood before my eyes,
and I heard a hushed voice: "Can a mortal be more righteous than God?
Can a man be more pure than his Maker?"

JOB 4:15-17

Just as Elijah was spoken to by God in a "still, small voice" on Mount Horeb, Eliphaz the Temanite "heard a hushed voice" (Job 4:16). In other versions, "still small voice" (KJV) is translated "a gentle whisper" (NIV) and "a sound of sheer silence" (NRSV). Each expression places the emphasis on the *unobtrusiveness* of the way God communicated. God used this unassuming way rather than in the earthquake, wind and fire, and Elijah was wise enough to recognize this unpretentious communication (1 Kings 19:11-13).

The still, small voice of God bears the stamp of his personality quite clearly and is given in a way we can learn to recognize. In contrast with hearing God in Scripture, dreams, visions or extraordinary events, the *medium* through which the still, small voice comes is diminished almost to the vanishing point.

REFLECT: *Ponder these phrases: hushed voice; still, small voice; gentle whisper; sound of sheer silence. What do you make of an almighty Creator who chooses to speak this way? What needs to happen within you so you can recognize such unpretentious communication?*

Only Other People!

Elijah was a man just like us. He prayed earnestly that it would not rain,
and it did not rain on the land for three and a half years.
Again he prayed, and the heavens gave rain, and the earth produced its crops.

JAMES 5:17-18

Try to read the biblical accounts as if what is described is happening to *us*. We must make a conscious effort to think that such things *might* happen to us and to imagine what it would be like if they did.

This can be difficult because we tend to think that God does marvelous things only with *other* people. But Elijah, Moses and Paul were like us, subject to "like passions" as we are (James 5:17 KJV). When misunderstood or mistreated, they felt as we would feel. They experienced hunger, weariness, nervousness, confusion and fear just as we do. They doubted their abilities and self-worth just as we do. Just like us—witness Moses and Gideon—they often said, "Oh, no! Not *me*. I can't do it."

PRAY: *Choose a biblical character you may have put on a pedestal so that you don't believe he or she had "like passions" to yours. Think of reasons he or she might have been afraid, frustrated, defensive or resentful. Thank God for this human who responded to him, and ask the Spirit to live in you as you respond to God.*

M O N D A Y *The Mind of Christ*

But we have the mind of Christ.

1 CORINTHIANS 2:16

How can simple humans "have the mind of Christ"? The apostle Paul begins by saying that "no one knows the thoughts of God except the *Spirit of God*" (1 Corinthians 2:11, emphasis added). But because we have received the Spirit of God, we understand the things of God: "We have not received the spirit of the world but the Spirit who is from God, that we may understand what God has freely given us" (v. 12). So it is possible for us to use God's Spirit, which we have received, to search the mind of God. After quoting Isaiah's question that seems unanswerable, "For who has known the mind of the Lord that he may instruct him?" (Isaiah 40:13), Paul replies in thankful celebration: "But we have the mind of Christ." This equips us to be in the process of coming to know the mind of God.

MEDITATE: *Read again the words of 1 Corinthians 2:11, 12, 16 above. Relish the idea that God has given you his Spirit so that you may understand the things of God (v. 12) and have the "mind of Christ" (v. 16). Don't worry about fully under-standing this mysterious truth. Simply delight in the idea of it, as best you can.*

TUESDAY   *Union with God*

> *I pray also for those who will believe in me through their message,*
> *that all of them may be one, Father, just as you are in me and I am in you.*

JOHN 17:20-21

God uses our spirit's knowledge of ourselves, heightened by his presence and direction, to search us out and reveal to us truth about ourselves and our world. And we are able to use God's knowledge of himself—made available to us through the Holy Spirit as well as Christ and the Scriptures—to understand in some measure *his* thoughts and intentions toward us and to help us see his workings in our world (1 Corinthians 2:9-16).

In the communion of the believer with God, their two beings are unified and inhabit each other, just as Jesus prayed: "I ask . . . that they may all be one. As you, Father, are in me and I am in you, may they also be in us" (John 17:20-21 NRSV). As this union grows, God's laws increasingly form the foundation of our hearts; his love is our love, his faith our faith.

REFLECT: *As God's way of thinking forms the foundation of our hearts, it's as if we put on a headset that helps us think as God thinks. How has your thinking changed to resemble the way God thinks? How would you like it to change further?*

Search Me, O God!

The spirit of man is the candle of the LORD,
searching all the inward parts of the belly.

PROVERBS 20:27 KJV

Form a picture of God walking through your personality, using your spirit as a candle, directing your attention to one thing after another. Your goal is to cooperate with God and pray, "Bring the light to bear upon my life, please." This is similar to how we might go to a doctor and say, "Examine me, please, and see if corrections to my physical condition are needed. Find out what is wrong and repair it."

We can more easily invite God to do this as we truly believe that he is friendly and helpful. It's not frightening that God desires to straighten, inform and correct for our good because it's also to comfort and encourage us. As we believe that he really does love us, then we can begin to pray heartily with the psalmist, "Search me, O God, and know my heart; test me and know my anxious thoughts" (Psalm 139:23).

PRAY: *Speak to God about whether you truly believe that he desires to be friendly and helpful. That he desires to straighten, inform and correct for our good. That he really does love us and is therefore safe to search us. Then, if you can, pray, "Bring the light of the candle of the Lord to bear upon my life, please."*

I the LORD search the heart and examine the mind,
to reward a man according to his conduct,
according to what his deeds deserve.

JEREMIAH 17:10

Recurring thoughts are important in God's communication with us, as Russ Johnston points out in *How to Know the Will of God:*

> We would see wonderful results if we would deal with the thoughts that continue in our minds in a godly manner. But most people don't. . . . As thoughts come into your mind and continue, ask God, "Do you really want me (or us) to do this?" Most of us just let those thoughts collapse— and God looks for someone else to stand in the gap.

These recurring thoughts touch on every part of the self: family, possessions, profession and health; one's fear of death; attitudes toward God; sexuality; preoccupation with reputation; concern with appearance and countless other areas of one's life. Although recurring thoughts are not *always* an indication that God is speaking, they are not to be lightly disregarded.

P R A Y : *Sit quietly before God and ponder what recurring thoughts have come to you lately regarding the areas listed above. No matter how mundane these thoughts seem, bring them before God and ask him to help you see a next step, however small, you could take to act on them. This might be asking someone a question or writing a note.*

Trustworthy Thoughts?

Do not conform any longer to the pattern of this world,
but be transformed by the renewing of your mind.

ROMANS 12:2

But can we trust our thoughts? Aren't most thoughts inherently bad? Since God said, "For my thoughts are not your thoughts" (Isaiah 55:8), doesn't that mean that if a thought is *our* thought, it cannot possibly be trusted? After all, our hearts are desperately wicked, beyond our powers of comprehension (Jeremiah 17:9).

It's true that God's view of things often differs from the view of the normal person apart from God. But this point must not obscure the simple fact that God comes to us precisely in and through our thoughts, perceptions and experiences. Since this is the substance of our lives, God can approach our conscious life *only* through them. We are, therefore, to be transformed by the *renewing of our minds* (Romans 12:2). God's gracious incursions into our souls can make our thoughts his thoughts. He will help us learn to distinguish when a thought is ours alone and when it is also his.

PRAY: *Consider what you've thought about today and yesterday. Stop and prayerfully ask God if the "candle of the Lord" is searching you or if the thoughts have some other significance (Proverbs 20:27). Then invite God to invade certain parts of you (name them) and gently conform you to the beauty of his ways.*

God Speaks Today

Do not quench the Spirit. Do not despise the words of prophets,
but test everything; hold fast to what is good; abstain from every form of evil.

1 THESSALONIANS 5:19-22 NRSV

There is no foundation in Scripture why God might not speak through angels, dreams, visions, an audible voice, a human voice or the still, small voice in our thoughts. No one should be alarmed or thrown into doubt by having such experiences or by hearing reports that other people have experienced them. As always, we should follow Paul's admonition not to quench the Spirit or despise the prophets' words. We do test everything, but *hold fast* to what is good (1 Thessalonians 5:19-22).

It is true that the existence of the church and the presence of the full written Scripture give new dimensions to the way in which God deals with human beings. But nothing *in* Scripture indicates that the biblical modes of God's communication with humans have been superseded or abolished by either the presence of the church or the close of the scriptural canon.

PRAY: *Think of someone who has had an experience that has alarmed you—perhaps a dream or vision. Ask God to show you how to come alongside this brother or sister. Do you need to listen with more encouragement? With more insightfulness? Do you need to ask more questions or to ask fewer questions?*

M O N D A Y

Woe to those who are wise in their own eyes and clever in their own sight. . . .
Their roots will decay and their flowers blow away like dust;
for they have rejected the law of the LORD Almighty.

ISAIAH 5:21, 24

God continues to address his children in most of the ways he addressed biblical characters. Testimonies of hearing God from honest, clear-minded and devout followers (including many of the greatest Christians throughout the ages) shouldn't be discarded. Of course, fakery and confusion do occur, well intended and not, but a blank, dogmatic denial that God still speaks to us has no scriptural foundation.

Moreover, denying that God speaks is often an attempt to substitute safety and deadness for living communications from God. Other times it's a preference to look to ponderous scholars or letter-learned scribes to interpret God's word rather than hearing the voice that is available to people even of the plainest sort. Still other times, it's a way of resigning oneself to hear only what one has heard before instead of listening for the specific word he might have for one today.

REFLECT: *Have you in any way attempted to substitute safety and deadness for specific living communications from God? Do you need to give God permission to say anything to you that you need to hear in any way he chooses to speak?*

From General to Specific

Do not merely listen to the word, and so deceive yourselves. Do what it says.
Anyone who listens to the word but does not do what it says is like a man who
looks at his face in a mirror and, after looking at himself,
goes away and immediately forgets what he looks like.

JAMES 1:22-24

The close of the scriptural canon marks the point in the ongoing divine-human conversation where the principles and doctrines of Christian faith and practice are so adequately stated that nothing more need be said *in general*. Biblical Christians believe that God will say nothing further to extend or contradict those principles.

But the principles of the faith have to be applied before they can be lived out. Our reverence for and faith in the Bible must not blind us to our need for personal divine instruction *within the principles of the Bible yet beyond the details of what it explicitly says*.

MEDITATE: *Read James 1:22-25. Picture yourself reading Scripture in an obligatory, half-attentive way without asking God to speak to you today. Feel the pain of this behavior and how it resembles that of the one who "looks at his face in a mirror and . . . goes away and immediately forgets." What do you wish to pray for yourself concerning your need for divine personal instruction about the details of your life?*

Necessities for Life with God

His divine power has given us everything we need for life and godliness
through our knowledge of him who called us by his own glory and goodness.

2 PETER 1:3

Let's consider the argument that voices, visions, dreams, prophetic people or individual thoughts as communications from God are no longer needed because the Bible and the church now speak for God. If by what is "needed" we mean what is minimally required for humans to know God, this, according to the Bible itself, is available without the Bible and the church: "For what can be known about God is plain to them, because God has shown it to them. Ever since the creation of the world his eternal power and divine nature, invisible though they are, have been understood" (Romans 1:19-21 NRSV). Yet God thought creation was not enough, so he gave us the Bible and the church.

However, if by what is "needed" we mean what is required for a redemptive, personal *relationship* between God and the individual, then the mere existence of the Bible and the church is not enough. Besides existing, they must function in people's lives. For this to happen they must become the means through which God personally and uniquely addresses each individual.

P R A Y : *Thank God for all he has given you "for life and godliness," that you may know him and sense his call to his glory and goodness.*

Moderns Are Better Off?

What has been will be again, what has been done will be done again;
there is nothing new under the sun. Is there anything of which one can say,
"Look! This is something new"? It was here already, long ago; it was here before our time.

ECCLESIASTES 1:9-10

Answering the query that miracles and gifts of the Spirit were only for the apostolic church, Andrew Murray (1828-1917) dismissed the idea that such a particularized presence of the hand of God was only necessary in the early days of Christianity: "Ah, no! What about the power of heathenism even today wherever the gospel seeks to combat it, even in our *modern society,* and in the midst of the ignorance and unbelief which reigns even in the Christian nations?"

An amazing conceit that frequently creeps into the church is that we are so much better off now than in more primitive times. Now we need only the written Word of God without the divine presence and interaction with humanity described in that written Word. How obviously mistaken this is today, as biblical truth and ideas serve less and less to guide the course of human events.

REFLECT: *What is at the root of these ideas: I live in spiritually enlightened times; I can get by without as much spiritual help as others need? How do we hurt ourselves with these ideas?*

F R I D A Y

Praise the LORD, O my soul, and forget not all his benefits.

PSALM 103:2

By thinking our times have progressed since the days of early Christianity (and so God's guidance isn't now necessary), we shut ourselves off from God's resources for life and ministry in the present. C. H. Spurgeon is right on the mark with his comments on Psalm 103:2 found in *Morning by Morning:*

> We do our Lord an injustice when we suppose that He wrought all His mighty acts, and showed Himself strong for those in the early time, but doth not perform wonders or lay bare His arm for the saints who are now upon the earth. Let us review our own lives. Surely in these we may discover some happy incidents, refreshing to ourselves and glorifying to our God. Have you had no deliverances? Have you passed through no rivers, supported by the divine presence? Have you walked through no fires unharmed? Have you had no manifestations? Have you had no choice favours? . . . Surely the goodness of God has been the same to us as to the saints of old.

P R AY : *Talk to your soul (as the psalmist did above and in many other psalms) and remind it of how God has benefited the parts of you that your soul organizes: your will, your thoughts, your feelings, your body.*

Bible Deism

The Sadducees say that there is no resurrection,
and that there are neither angels nor spirits,
but the Pharisees acknowledge them all.

ACTS 23:8

Classical deism, associated with the extreme rationalism of the sixteenth to eighteenth centuries, held that God created his world complete and then went away, leaving humanity to its own devices. God made no individualized intervention in the lives of human beings. "Bible deism" then would hold that God gave us the Bible and then went away, leaving us to make what we could of it, with no individualized communication through the Bible or otherwise. The results of Bible deism in believers today are very much like what took place with the Sadducees in the text above: they did not accept individual communications with God, and they didn't believe in angels, the resurrection or an afterlife. This is an unbiblical view and harms our ability to live as God's children.

REFLECT: *How do the attributes of God—a personal being, omnipotent, loving and so on—contradict Bible deism, the belief that now that we have the Bible, God has gone away and left us to make what we can out of it without communicating with us through the Bible or otherwise?*

M O N D A Y

Helping Others

> *I will lead the blind by ways they have not known,*
> *along unfamiliar paths I will guide them;*
> *I will turn the darkness into light before them and make the rough places smooth.*
> *These are the things I will do; I will not forsake them.*

ISAIAH 42:16

One of the greatest harms we can do to those who look up to us spiritually—new believers, family members, friends—is to express doubts that God will meet them personally or that any interaction with God they have must have our stamp of approval. If our gospel does not free the individual for a unique life of spiritual adventure in living with God daily, we simply have not entered fully into the good news that Jesus brought.

Of course there are dangers in encouraging people to hear from God. People do go off the deep end, and this problem must be addressed. Yet trouble also comes from going off the *shallow* end, and so we must lead people to understand the voice of God and how it works in their lives.

PRAY: *Use phrases in Isaiah 42:16 to pray for those you are helping along the way of God: lead them by ways they have not known; guide them along unfamiliar paths; turn the darkness into light before them; make the rough places smooth. Ask God for help in partnering with him to help others this way.*

Words Come to Life

> For the word of God is living and active.
> Sharper than any double-edged sword,
> it penetrates even to dividing soul and spirit, joints and marrow;
> it judges the thoughts and attitudes of the heart.

HEBREWS 4:12

One of the most damaging things we can do to people's spiritual prospects is to suggest that God will *not* deal with them specifically, personally, intelligibly and consciously or that they cannot *count on* him to do so, as he knows best. Once we have conveyed this idea to them, it makes no sense to attempt to lead them into a personal relationship with God.

A biblical Christian is not just someone who holds certain beliefs *about* the Bible. He or she is also someone who *leads the kind of life demonstrated* in the Bible: a life of personal, intelligent interaction with God.

MEDITATE: *Read Hebrews 4:12. Consider how interpreters of this verse often restrict its meaning to a negative searchlight activity of our faulty thoughts. How do the phrases "living and active" and "penetrates even to [innermost parts]" take on a desirable, even exciting tone when applied to counting on God to deal with us specifically, personally, intelligibly and consciously? And when applied to living a life of personal, intelligent interaction with God?*

Asking for Help

> *Abraham said[,] "The LORD, the God of heaven, who brought me out of my*
> *father's household and my native land and who spoke to me and promised me on oath,*
> *saying, 'To your offspring I will give this land'—he will send his angel before you*
> *so that you can get a wife for my son from there."*

GENESIS 24:67

How wonderful that Abraham could assure his puzzled servant that God was guiding him back to the city of Nahor to find a wife for Isaac (Genesis 24:1-7)! How wonderful that the servant could come to an utterly new understanding of God because he *did* experience guidance and was, indeed, guided into knowledge of guidance itself. He learned by experience to work with our God *who is available.*

Recognizing God's voice is something we must *learn to do through our own personal experience and experimentation.* Others more advanced on the Way can help us identify the voice of God and instruct us in how to respond.

MEDITATE: *Read as much of Genesis 24 as you have time for. (The drama stretches from vv. 1-61, but you can stop before the end.) Put yourself in the place of Abraham's chief servant in every scene. What do you learn about trusting God for guidance?*

THURSDAY

The Listener's Maturity

As soon as Jesus was baptized, he went up out of the water.
At that moment heaven was opened, and he saw the Spirit of God descending like a dove
and lighting on him. And a voice from heaven said,
"This is my Son, whom I love; with him I am well pleased."

MATTHEW 3:16-17

As Bible history proceeds, we notice that the more mature the listener is, the more clear the message from God is. Also, as the maturity of the listener increases, the role of dreams, visions and other strange phenomena and altered states decreases.

In the lives of New Testament personalities—especially Jesus himself—there is a great deal of strictly spiritual—nonphysical—communication between God and his people. Visions, dreams and angels continue to play some part—as they may today. When these phenomena were the main (as opposed to occasional) means of interaction, it indicated a *less developed spiritual life in the individual or in the group.* This is not to be judgmental, but to point out that we should expect to grow into the kind of life with God in which we hear from him amid frequent times of conversational prayer.

REFLECT: *When you pray, do you ever have a conversation with God? If not, how might you modify your times of prayer to help that happen? If so, what sorts of things have you been hearing from God lately?*

The Priority of the Voice

> *When a prophet of the LORD is among you,*
> *I reveal myself to him in visions, I speak to him in dreams.*
> *But this is not true of my servant Moses. . . .*
> *With him I speak face to face, clearly and not in riddles;*
> *he sees the form of the LORD.*

NUMBERS 12:6-8

Moses' brother and sister, Aaron and Miriam, were jealous of how God spoke to Moses, so God called them into the meeting tent and spoke to them. God spoke to Moses "not in riddles." Riddles are obscure, barely intelligible sayings on a par with the gibberish of "mediums and spiritists, who whisper and mutter" (Isaiah 8:19). We cannot know for sure what riddles mean, and they provide a fertile field for wild conjectures and manipulative interpretations.

Many who claim to speak for God refer to their visions and dreams or to vague impressions or feelings. They can articulate no clear, sane meaning. This does not mean that they have *not* truly been spoken to. But Moses was spoken to directly. Therefore when he spoke for God he was always specific, precise and clear. This is what we aspire to.

REFLECT: *What is needed in your character for God to trust you as he trusted Moses? Do you need more Moses-like humility—lack of pride and self-sufficiency (Numbers 12:3)? More confidence in God (Hebrews 11:24)?*

> *"Abba, Father," he said, "everything is possible for you.*
> *Take this cup from me. Yet not what I will, but what you will."*

MARK 14:36

The voice is the preferred encounter with God rather than such things as dreams or visions. That voice may be the audible voice, the human voice or the still, small voice within the silence of our minds. Its superiority lies in two things: the *clarity* of its content and the *advanced spiritual condition* of those who can hear and receive it.

In *The Way*, E. Stanley Jones, who practiced interaction with God's voice, writes:

> Jesus was supreme sanity. He went off into no visions, no dreams. He got His guidance through prayer as you and I do. He got guidance when in control of His faculties, and not when out of control as in dreams. I do not say that God may not guide through a vision or dream; but if He does, it will be seldom, and it will be because He cannot get hold of our normal processes to guide them. God is found most clearly and benefi- cially in the normal rather than in the abnormal. Jesus is the Normal, for He is the Norm.

REFLECT: *How do you respond to the idea that Jesus got his guidance through prayer as you and I do? Is this surprising? Empowering? What does it lead you to want to do?*

MONDAY *Seeking the Spectacular*

The Pharisees came and began to question Jesus.
To test him, they asked him for a sign from heaven. He sighed deeply and said,
"Why does this generation ask for a miraculous sign?
I tell you the truth, no sign will be given to it."

MARK 8:11-12

The more spectacular encounters with God generally go along with the *less mature* levels of the spiritual life. (Yet the absence of spectacular events must not be taken as indicating great spiritual development. Such an absence is also consistent with utter deadness.) It is well that this should be so. The spectacular encounters are obscure in their content and meaning, perhaps for our protection.

When people *seek* the spectacular, it is because of childishness in their personality. Children love the spectacular and show themselves as children by actively seeking it out, running heedlessly after it. It may sometimes be given by God—it may be necessary—because of our denseness or our hardheartedness. However, it is never to be taken as a mark of spiritual adulthood or superiority.

MEDITATE: *Read Mark 8:11-12. Keep in mind that although Jesus gladly used signs of healing and feeding and later confirmed the word of the disciples with signs, he was not glad in this scene. He "sighed deeply." The Pharisees were seeking the spectacular. What do you think Jesus would have preferred they sought?*

Speaking of the Spectacular

I know a man in Christ who fourteen years ago
was caught up to the third heaven.
Whether it was in the body or out of the body I do not know—God knows.
And I know that this man—whether in the body or apart
from the body I do not know, but God knows—
was caught up to paradise. He heard inexpressible things,
things that man is not permitted to tell.

2 CORINTHIANS 12:2-4

If spectacular things do come to them, those who are more advanced in the Way of Christ never lightly discuss them or invoke them to prove that they are right or "with it" in some special way. Many think that Paul was speaking of himself as the one "caught up in the third heaven." But he would not identify himself that way or tell anything about it. No doubt God was the one he spoke to about it.

PRAY: *Think of something that has occurred between God and you that is inspiring. Since God is the one to talk to about these things, do so now, perhaps beginning with "Remember when . . ." If you're not sure what to bring to God, talk to him about the moment of your birth. Recount what details you've heard about, knowing that God knows all the details and treasures that day.*

Headed in the Right Direction

The path of the righteous is like the first gleam of dawn,
shining ever brighter till the full light of day.

PROVERBS 4:18

When God sends us dramatic "signs" along the way, we are grateful, but they are not the reality or the complete picture. They do tell us in which direction to head and keep us going on the right course. Bob Mumford, discussing in *Take Another Look at Guidance* the spectacular forms of communication from God, remarks:

> Signs are given to us, because God meets us on the level where we operate. . . . In guidance, when God shows us a sign, it doesn't mean we've received the final answer. A sign means we're on the way. On the highway we may pass a sign saying, "New York: 100 miles." The sign doesn't mean we've reached New York, but it tells us we're on the right road.

PRAY: *Consider how you need to pray regarding remarkable signs and signposts: to thank God for those given in the past; to ask for such signs for newcomers along the Way of Christ; to tell God that you are now more eager to be guided by conversation with him.*

THURSDAY

Christ's Abiding Presence

Abide in me as I abide in you.
Just as the branch cannot bear fruit by itself unless it abides in the vine,
neither can you unless you abide in me.

JOHN 15:4 NRSV

Who among us would really know what to do if the great God came down in splendor and somehow stood spectacularly before us? It makes us want to become more ready to be addressed by the still, small voice of Jesus! How good it is that God left the spectacular forms that had been necessary—and perhaps still are necessary for some purposes—and came to deal with us by the very whispers of his Spirit.

In *Take Another Look at Guidance,* Bob Mumford writes:

God wants to bring us beyond the point where we need signs to discern His guiding hand. Satan cannot counterfeit the peace of God or the love of God dwelling in us. When Christ's abiding presence becomes our guide, then guidance becomes an almost unconscious response to the gentle moving of His Holy Spirit within us.

MEDITATE: *Read John 15:4 and notice the rhythm of the words. It's as if you and Christ are moving together, as if you were skating or dancing arm in arm. You are so in sync with Christ that his next movements are plain to you—and you immediately follow. Ask God to help you live that way.*

The Quietness of Jesus

Here is my servant whom I have chosen, the one I love, in whom I delight;
I will put my Spirit on him, and he will proclaim justice to the nations.
He will not quarrel or cry out; no one will hear his voice in the streets.
A bruised reed he will not break, and a smoldering wick he will not snuff out,
till he leads justice to victory. In his name the nations will put their hope.

MATTHEW 12:18-21

The incarnate Son comes without strife, so gentle that his voice is not to be heard above the chatter of the street (Matthew 12:19). It is because of this approach that the Gentiles, or people generally, will finally come to have confidence in him.

I am so thankful for the quiet written Word, for the history and presence of the church of the Lamb, for the lives of the saints and for the tireless, still conquests of the Spirit of God. These approach me. These *I* can approach, and through them I can approach God while he safely draws ever closer to me.

MEDITATE: *Read Matthew 12:18-21. What words stand out to you? Contrast this picture of proclaiming "justice to the nations" with noisy television talk shows, ranting speeches and haggling lawsuits that supposedly persuade people to act justly. What quiet act of justice or hope is God leading you to do?*

For the kingdom of God is not a matter of eating and drinking,
but of righteousness, peace and joy in the Holy Spirit.

ROMANS 14:17

The rivals of God's still, small voice within—dreams, visions, phenomena—continue to be necessary and have their place. But once we earnestly seek God, we can move beyond the need to have big things happen to reassure us that somehow we are all right—and possibly that others are not. Then we begin to understand and rejoice that, as Jesus so clearly lived and taught, the life of the kingdom is "righteousness, peace and joy in the Holy Spirit" (Romans 14:17).

Then we begin to understand that God's whole purpose is to bring us to the point where he can walk with us quietly, calmly and constantly, leaving us space to grow to be his (often fumbling) colaborers. We will have some distance from him and yet be united with him because we are being conformed to the image of his Son, bearing the family resemblance.

REFLECT: *The readers of Romans were sidetracked into thinking that the kingdom consisted of eating and drinking the right things—items offered or not offered to idols. What good activities distract us from becoming people with whom God can walk quietly, calmly and constantly so that we experience the righteousness, peace and joy in the Holy Spirit in the kingdom of God?*

MONDAY *Conversing with God*

> *I will listen to what God the LORD will say;*
> *he promises peace to his people, his saints—*
> *but let them not return to folly.*

PSALM 85:8

In *Prayer: Conversing with God*, Rosalind Rinker relates how, after years of missionary service and an unsatisfactory prayer life, she found herself rebellious and spiritually empty. Then, through a serious illness and other difficulties, "God began to take care of my rebellions through his great love. He began to teach me to listen to his voice."

Almost by "chance," as she was praying with a friend, she interrupted her friend's prayer with thanksgiving on a point that was being prayed for. After a moment of awkward silence, they laughed. They settled down again to prayer but now "with a sense of joy, . . . of the Lord's presence very near." They prayed: "Should we give Thee more opportunity as we are praying to get Thy ideas through to us?" Then Rinker stopped praying and said to her friend, "I believe the Lord taught us something just now! Instead of each of us making a prayer-speech to Him, let's talk things over with Him, including Him in it, as we do when we have a conversation."

REFLECT: *Have you lapsed into making "prayer-speeches" at God? What sort of prayer enhances your life with God? How might "talking things over with him" move people away from rebellion and folly?*

TUESDAY *God Always Responds*

I wait for you, O LORD;
you will answer, O Lord my God.

PSALM 38:15

In a conversational relationship with God, God may not give us what we ask for, but he always *responds* in some way. We commonly say a prayer was answered only when we are *granted* our requests. When a request is denied, does this mean that God has not responded?

Some people say that God's answer is silence in these cases, but if we know how to listen, God will normally *tell* us something when he does not grant our requests. We will hear it and grow through it if we have learned to recognize his voice.

When Paul begged the Lord to remove his "thorn in the flesh," God did turn down the request, but God was not silent: *"But his answer was: 'My grace is all you need; power is most fully seen in weakness'"* (2 Corinthians 12:9 NEB, emphasis added). God is not impassive, like an unresponsive pagan idol; he calls us to grow into a life of personal interchange with him that does justice to the idea of our being his children.

PRAY: *Think back to your "unanswered" prayers. How did God respond to you to build goodness and peace in you? Then pray Psalm 38:15. Notice the willingness to wait ("I wait for you") and the confidence that God would respond ("you will answer").*

Now we see but a poor reflection as in a mirror;
then we shall see face to face.
Now I know in part; then I shall know fully, even as I am fully known.

1 C O R I N T H I A N S 1 3 : 1 2

God often speaks to us in obscure ways to allow us the room and time we need to respond. He lets us know he is speaking to us but also that we need to stretch out in growth in order to receive the message. Perhaps we think, "God, why don't you just say it? Tell me in detail how to live." But we are usually full of mistaken ideas about what that would actually mean. If it actually happened, it would probably kill us or unbalance us. So God in his mercy continues to approach us obliquely. Our minds and values have to be restructured, but God speaks anyway because he appreciates our interests. As we mature, this is less so, until that time when we can safely know him as he knows us (1 Corinthians 13:12).

P R A Y : *Thank God for speaking to you obliquely so you have time and room to respond. Ask God how your mind and values need to be restructured so that you can hear the fullness of what he's saying to you. Delight in the future moment when you will "know fully."*

A man's steps are directed by the LORD.
How then can anyone understand his own way?

PROVERBS 20:24

Some people feel discouraged because they have to struggle to understand what God is saying to them. Even focusing on the Bible requires persistent and energetic work to understand it. But such struggle is not inappropriate; it is natural and right. Struggling to understand is normal. A truism of life is that in its most important moments we don't have the foggiest idea of what we are doing. Our ignorance is partly for our own good. Did you *really* know what was happening when you entered the university or military training, got married or brought a child into the world? In some vague sense you did, but you also had little idea of what it meant in the long run. If you had understood all that it meant at the time, you probably would not have had the courage to proceed. Then you would have missed out on much good that has come to you through those events.

REFLECT: *Describe your level of frustration with not really knowing what is going on at times: very frustrated; accepting that you don't know; not feeling like you have to know; being downright grateful that you don't know, as long as God knows; maybe everything's okay.*

> They replied, "Let one of us sit at your right and
> the other at your left in your glory."
> "You don't know what you are asking," Jesus said.
> "Can you drink the cup I drink or be baptized with the baptism I am baptized with?"
> "We can," they answered.
> Jesus said to them, "You will drink the cup I drink and be
> baptized with the baptism I am baptized with."

MARK 10:37-39

James and John came to Jesus asking, in effect, to be vice president and secretary of state when he became president. When Jesus pointed out they had no idea what they were asking, they told him to "bring it on." James was the first apostle to be martyred. John was tortured with hot oil (according to tradition) and exiled on the barren island of Patmos, where he received a revelation of Jesus Christ.

This was not what James and John had in mind, but they grew to the vision and the task as they stepped forward in faith. They lived and died as friends and colaborers of Jesus.

MEDITATE: *Read Mark 10:37-39, wondering at how little James and John guessed. Don't view them as forward and uninformed, but as ripe persons God could use. Consider that your not knowing what's going on doesn't mean God isn't using you or honoring you; instead it equips you to be used.*

The Word of God and the Rule of God

Where the word of a king is, there is power.

ECCLESIASTES 8:4 KJV

The phrase "still, small voice" might seem to suggest that what lies at the heart of a relationship with God is something weak and marginal. But that is far from the truth. One who hears God's voice is operating from the foundation and framework of all reality, not from the fringe.

This is true because God uses the words of his voice to do the work of creating, of ruling and of redeeming. To hear the words of God's voice is to be in relationship with God as a colaborer in the work of creating, ruling and redeeming.

REFLECT: *Think of a time when you said words to someone that had a redemptive effect—they pulled that person out of sin and despair or renewed that person's being or helped him or her see truth. Thank God for allowing you to be a colaborer in using words of redemption.*

M O N D A Y   *A Piece of God's Mind*

> *The secret things belong to the LORD our God,*
> *but the things revealed belong to us and to our children forever,*
> *that we may follow all the words of this law.*

DEUTERONOMY 29:29

If you find words written on a wall or overhear them spoken in a crowd, you cannot tell whose words they are and so the meaning is blurred. Without being tied to its speaker or writer, a word is only a sound or a mark on a page. But when a word is tied to its speaker or writer, it is an expression of that person's *self*. It reveals his or her thoughts and intentions.

To understand the meaning of God's words, we must understand the *meaning given to them by God*—the thoughts, feelings or actions God associates with the words and plans to convey to us. By giving us his words, God literally gives us a piece of his mind. Through his words we may know his thoughts and feelings and share in the life of God.

MEDITATE: *Ponder Deuteronomy 29:29. Consider how all knowledge and secrets belong to God, but he chooses to reveal certain secret things (a piece of his mind) to humans for our good. What do such ideas make you want to pray? What do you wish to request or want God to know about your desires?*

T U E S D A Y

The Spiritual Power of Words

Death and life are in the power of the tongue.

PROVERBS 18:21 KJV

Through words, soul impacts soul, sometimes with a great spiritual force. As written marks or sounds alone, words are nothing. It is their mental side, their spiritual force, that hooks into the hidden levers of mind and reality and gives them their immense power. If we do not understand Spanish or Greek, we hear the sounds, but they have little or no effect because they are without meaning for us.

The true view of the power of words is forcefully given in the book of Proverbs: "Death and life are in the power of the tongue" (18:21 KJV); "Through patience a ruler can be persuaded, and a gentle tongue can break a bone" (25:15). This theme is carried into the New Testament. James remarks that the tongue is "a small member, yet it boasts of great exploits. How great a forest is set ablaze by a small fire!" (James 3:5 NRSV).

PRAY: *Consider the upcoming events of your day (or of tomorrow). Pray that the words you speak will impact others' souls with life (Proverbs 18:21) or even gentle persuasiveness if needed (25:15). Hold your hands over your lips and offer all of today's (or tomorrow's) words to God.*

 *Revealing Ourselves*

> *But the things that come out of the mouth come from the heart,*
> *and these make a man "unclean." For out of the heart come evil thoughts,*
> *murder, adultery, sexual immorality, theft, false testimony, slander.*
> *These are what make a man "unclean";*
> *but eating with unwashed hands does not make him "unclean."*

MATTHEW 15:18-20

The power of the word lies in the personality it conveys: "A gentle tongue is a tree of life, but perverseness in it breaks the spirit" (Proverbs 15:4 NRSV). Jesus regarded words as a direct revelation of our inner being: "For by your words you will be justified, and by your words you will be condemned" (Matthew 12:37 NRSV).

Children learn to say, "Sticks and stones may break my bones, but words can never hurt me." Adults teach them to say this in order to ease the pain that is inflicted on them by the meanness conveyed in the words of their playmates. How deeply people can be scarred by malicious or mindless chatter.

REFLECT: *Think about phrases such as "I was caught off-guard" or "I spoke before I thought." How possible is it that "the things that come out of the mouth come from the heart" and so our casual, random words reveal the parts of ourselves we're not proud of?*

Words as Spiritual Forces

It is the spirit that gives life; the flesh is useless.
The words that I have spoken to you are spirit and life.

JOHN 6:63 NRSV

Scripture is clear that words are spiritual forces. When Jesus' followers were struggling to understand his teaching on the bread of life and were overemphasizing the material realm (physical bread), Jesus said to them that the *words* he spoke to them were "spirit and life." Through his words Jesus imparted *himself*, his Spirit and his life. In some measure he also imparted the powers of God's sovereign rule to those who received his words. Through Jesus they "have tasted the goodness of the word of God and the powers of the age to come" (Hebrews 6:5 NRSV). This imparted power is referred to in Jesus' later explanation that "if you abide in me, and my words abide in you, ask for whatever you wish, and it will be done for you" (John 15:7 NRSV).

MEDITATE: *Read Jesus' sermon on the bread of life in John 6:32-58. Read slowly, remembering that through these words Jesus is imparting himself to you. Don't be frustrated if you don't fully understand them, but do your best to "receive" them. When you're finished, consider that you have tasted the goodness of God and the powers of the age to come.*

The heavens declare the glory of God;
the skies proclaim the work of his hands.
Day after day they pour forth speech; night after night they display knowledge.
There is no speech or language where their voice is not heard.
Their voice goes out into all the earth, their words to the ends of the world.

PSALM 19:1-4

The *word of God* is God speaking and communicating. When God speaks, he expresses his mind, his character and his purposes. Thus he is always present with his word.

But words of God are more than "words," as we think of them. *All expressions of God's mind* are "words" of God. Anything God does to express his mind are "words" of God. This is true whether God uses things that are *outside* the human mind (as in natural phenomena expressed in Psalm 19:1-4, other human beings, the incarnate Christ—the Logos—or the Bible) or *inside* the human mind (our own thoughts, intentions and feelings). God creates, rules and redeems through these words.

MEDITATE: *Read Psalm 19:1-4 above. Respond to God about how these words express the mind, character and purposes of God. Are you surprised that nature is a "word" of God?*

A Kingdom of Words

In these last days [God] has spoken to us by his Son,
whom he appointed heir of all things, and through whom he made the universe.
The Son is the radiance of God's glory and the exact representation of his being,
sustaining all things by his powerful word.

HEBREWS 1:2-3

Many people believe the universe is a place in which only certain physical or mechanical relationships exist between things. Blind forces cause physical objects to push and pull among each other. This naturalistic outlook cannot help us understand human beings, culture or the religious life.

In contrast, the outlook that identifies with the mind of Christ and with living life in Christ's footsteps is one that sees the universe as a *kingdom*. A kingdom does not work merely by mechanical moves, such as pushes and pulls. Essentially it works by a king *communicating* thoughts and intentions through words or symbols. A kingdom is a network of personal relationships. In the kingdom of God, words are primary.

REFLECT: *Put yourself in a fanciful state of mind and consider what the world would be like if every thought in your mind automatically resulted in words and then powerful actions! We can be glad, of course, that this is not reality, but consider what this shows you about the dynamics of the mind of God. Then consider Christ "sustaining all things by his powerful word."*

MONDAY *Creation by Words*

> *And God said, "Let there be lights in the dome of the sky. . . .*
> *Let the waters bring forth swarms of living creatures. . . .*
> *Let the earth bring forth living creatures of every kind. . . .*
> *Let us make humankind in our image, according to our likeness."*

GENESIS 1:14, 20, 24, 26 NRSV

God created the heavens and the earth by speaking it forth using a sequence of directly creative words. God's first creative act was to create light, a form of physical energy (Genesis 1:3). How did he create light? He *spoke words:* "Let there be light." God's speaking—the word of God—is the expression of his mind.

The creation of light and the result (light itself) are both to be viewed as words of God. The writer of Hebrews emphasizes God's speech and the Son's word in creation: after *speaking* through the prophets, God *spoke* through his Son, who then sustains everything by his *word* (Hebrews 1:1-3).

PRAY: *Consider how God's word creates, accomplishes and moves things around. With this power of God's word in mind, offer requests that you have prayed many times before. You may wish to preface each request with, "Just as you said, 'Let there be light,' now, O God, say, 'Let . . .'"*

TUESDAY　　　　*The Finite Human*

Great is our Lord, and of great power: his understanding is infinite.

PSALM 147:5 KJV

Let's say you wanted to create a bouquet of flowers or a chocolate cake. You couldn't just think or say, "Let there be a bouquet!" or "Let there be a chocolate cake!" as God said, "Let there be light!" This is the meaning of our finiteness, which means limitation or *restriction*. You and I are under some restrictions regarding how we can make a cake. We must work with and through the eggs, the flour, the sugar, the heat of the oven and time passing. We must adapt ourselves and our actions to our ingredients and equipment. They dictate the order and limitations of our actions.

God, by contrast, operates without these restrictions or limits. He dictates the structure and order in all things. God's power and even God's self is infinite—boundless and continuing forever. If God wanted to say, "Let there be a bouquet!" or "Let there be a chocolate cake!" those items would appear. He is not finite as we are.

PRAY: *Ponder the word* infinite *(without limitation or restriction) and then praise God for his infinite . . . Begin with* power, understanding, creativity *and name as many things as you can. Then acknowledge to God how finite you are in these same areas.*

> *But he is in one mind, and who can turn him?*
> *and what his soul desireth, even that he doeth.*

JOB 23:13 KJV

In our finite existence only two things resemble the immediate creative power of the *word* of God. One is the involuntary response of our body. Our body acts—reaching out to grab an object before it falls, smiling at the sight of a friend—so quickly that we don't realize we thought about it. The thought is there and our body obeys.

Another comparison would be our inward thoughts. After we have learned how to read music or weed a garden, we automatically act. We don't ask ourselves, "What is this musical note?" or "How do I pluck . . . ?" We intend to do, and do it.

God's word moves into action with this immediacy. Whatever God desires becomes his word and then becomes an action. This understanding that God's word *acts* gives us confidence that God can have a personal, powerful guiding relationship with us. God's words are never "just words," but power.

REFLECT: *Often your first thought about something is different from what you end up doing. You think you'll volunteer, but you change your mind and don't do it. What must be true about God that he doesn't think or change his mind, that "what his soul desireth, even that he doeth"?*

Natural Laws

> *Lasting to eternity, your word, Yahweh, unchanging in the heavens:*
> *your faithfulness lasts age after age; you founded the earth to endure.*
> *Creation is maintained by your rulings, since all things are your servants.*

PSALM 119:89-91 JB

The word of God—the thought and mind of God—continues to be present in the created universe, *upholding* it. What we call natural laws must be regarded as God's thoughts and intentions as to how the world should run. The events in the visible, material world—the unfolding of a rosebud, the germination of a seed, the conception and growth of a child, the evolution of galaxies—constitute a visible language manifesting not only a creative mind but, as Christian philosopher and Anglican bishop George Berkeley said long ago,

> a provident Governor, actually and intimately present, and attentive to all our interests and motions, who watches over our conduct and takes care of our minutest actions and designs throughout the whole course of our lives, informing, admonishing, and directing incessantly, in a most evident and sensible manner. (Mary W. Calkins, ed., *Berkeley: Essay, Principles and Dialogues with Selections from Other Writings*)

PRAY: *Go outdoors (or imagine yourself there) and note the natural laws in effect: a leaf falling from a tree, the sun or moon casting a shadow, scents passing through the air invisibly. Pray the verses above, noting that these effects are God's "rulings."*

FRIDAY

Human, but Still in Power

Jesus came and spake unto them, saying,
"All power is given unto me in heaven and in earth."

MATTHEW 28:18 KJV

At a certain point in history, God's word came to us through the womb of Mary: "He was in the world, and the world came into being through him; yet the world did not know him. He came to what was his own, and his people did not accept him" (John 1:10-11 NRSV). The *redemptive* entry of God upon the human scene was no intrusion into foreign territory; it was a move into "his own"—a focusing of that divine thought into the finite form of one human personality. Even there, the "control panel" of the entire universe was at hand. By voluntarily emptying himself during his incarnation (Philippians 2:7), Jesus refrained from all but a selective use of his power. Christ's "in-fleshment" was not an imposed restriction but rather the exercise of supreme power.

REFLECT: *How do you respond to the idea that Christ's coming to earth wasn't an imposed restriction but the exercise of the supreme power? How does this contradict notions that Jesus as a supreme being had to be squelched in order to become a baby? That Jesus endured being a victim to Roman powers? Picture such seemingly helpless moments in Jesus' life—his toddlerhood, his trial—but consider that even then all power was his in heaven and earth.*

SATURDAY / SUNDAY

Increasing Understanding

> *"I am the Alpha and the Omega," says the Lord God, "who is,*
> *and who was, and who is to come, the Almighty."*
>
> REVELATION 1 : 8

The New Testament is the story of increasing understanding of who Jesus was. Those among whom he was reared said, "This is Mary and Joseph's boy." His own disciples thought he might be Elijah or one of the old prophets risen from the dead. As Jesus quizzed the disciples on his identity, Peter announced in a flash of divine revelation, "You are the Messiah, the Son of the living God" (Matthew 16:16 NRSV).

Only in the later parts of the New Testament does the concept emerge of Jesus as a *cosmic* Messiah: a ruler spanning all geographical and ethnic differences, providing the glue of the universe (Colossians 1:17) and upholding all things by the word of his power (Hebrews 1:3). Thus he is, as described in the book of Revelation, the Alpha and Omega, the Faithful and True, the Word of God who leads the armies of heaven, the King of kings and Lord of lords.

REFLECT: *Consider how the true identity of Christ is unfolding in your life: logical and insightful teacher; redeemer of the world; powerful member of the community of the Trinity; cocreator and sustainer of the universe.*

Summer

M O N D A Y *Overwhelming Power*

> *"For my thoughts are not your thoughts, neither are your*
> *ways my ways," declares the LORD.*
> *"As the heavens are higher than the earth, so are my ways higher*
> *than your ways and my thoughts than your thoughts.*
> *As the rain and the snow come down from heaven, . . .*
> *so is my word that goes out from my mouth:*
> *It will not return to me empty, but will accomplish what I desire*
> *and achieve the purpose for which I sent it."*

ISAIAH 55:8-11

The word of God is characterized by overwhelming power, whether it is manifested in nature or in the incarnate Christ. *Words* of God are the expression of God's thoughts, which are as high above mere human thoughts as the heavens are above the earth. The power of the word coming out of God's mouth is like the powerful forces of nature—the rain and seed bringing forth plants, seed and bread to nourish the hungry (55:10). No wonder these words *will accomplish* what God desires!

MEDITATE: *Recall experiences of nature's power: forceful winds blowing lawn furniture around, water cascading from a dam, thunder and lightning waking you up at night, even the heat of sunbeams melting objects on a windowsill. Ponder the terror and the grandness of this power. Then transfer that sense to the word of God going forth.*

Unity of the Created Order

The voice of the LORD causes the oaks to whirl,
and strips the forest bare; and in his temple all say, "Glory!"
The LORD sits enthroned over the flood; the LORD sits enthroned as king forever.
May the LORD give strength to his people!

PSALM 29:9-11 NRSV

Psalm 29 shows how the natural order is unified with God's redemptive community under the word of God. Here God's voice causes trees and water to behave in certain ways. Still the Lord sits enthroned, giving strength to his people! The physical and spiritual are not isolated from each other.

This same unity is exhibited in the life of Jesus. He could turn water into wine, calm the billowing waves with his word and walk on them as on a pavement. But he could also place the word of God's kingdom rule into people's hearts, where it would bring forth fruit a hundredfold or sixtyfold or thirtyfold (Matthew 13:23). This is the word of God and the Son of God united in the ordering of the cosmos.

REFLECT: *How is your understanding that the word of God is so closely tied to nature? How do you respond to the idea that oaks and floodwaters respond to the voice of God and that when Jesus said, "Quiet! Be still!" the Sea of Galilee knew he was talking to it and responded?*

> *Since a king's word is supreme,*
> *who can say to him, "What are you doing?"*

E C C L E S I A S T E S   8 : 4

Understanding the power of words at the human level may help us understand the power of the creative word of God in *his* kingdom. ("For God is King over all the earth," Psalm 47:7). The writer of Ecclesiastes, himself a king, was amazed at what the word of a king could do.

Contrary to what is often thought, a king does *not* rule simply by brute force. The emperor Napoleon Bonaparte was about to use great force to subdue a certain population when a wise lieutenant said to him, "Monsignor, one cannot *sit* upon bayonets." This man understood that brute force could not lead to *settled* political rule. All government exists to some degree by consent of the governed. The ruler rules by words, understandings, allegiances and alliances—not just brute force.

Take away a king's authority and a king is like any other person. But when he is indeed kingly, his smallest word crushes enemies and prospers nations. In the kingdom of God, the creative word of God has even greater effects.

R E F L E C T : *Even though God is supreme and could force anyone to do anything, he works every day through words, understandings, allegiances and alliances. How have you seen God work that way?*

The Kingdom Works by Words

For I myself am a man under authority, with soldiers under me.
I tell this one, "Go," and he goes; and that one, "Come," and he comes.
I say to my servant, "Do this," and he does it.

LUKE 7:8

The Roman centurion seemed to understand, from his own experience of authority, how Jesus accomplished what he did. His practical faith in Jesus was based on his secular knowledge of the power of authoritative words. Even though he didn't seem to have any special degree of faith in God, he recognized Jesus' authority to heal. For him, Jesus' "speaking the word" was enough because where the *king's word* is, there is *power.* In his own arena the centurion was authorized to speak for a higher king, Caesar. The centurion understood what we often miss, because the kingdom of God *is* a kingdom; it works in large measure by words, as all kingdoms do. This understanding equipped him to have complete trust in Jesus' power.

MEDITATE: *Read Luke 7:1-10. Imagine yourself as a friend of the centurion telling Jesus not to come, but only to speak words of healing. Would you have trusted, as the centurion did, that you'd find the servant healed when you got back to the house? How well do you trust what God says? Would you prefer to see proof of God's care before believing it?*

F R I D A Y *Trusting God's Words*

> *When Jesus heard this, he was amazed at him,*
> *and turning to the crowd following him, he said,*
> *"I tell you, I have not found such great faith even in Israel."*

LUKE 7:9

Is it hard to believe that Jesus considered the centurion's faith greater than *anyone's* in Israel? What about John the Baptist? What about the shepherds and wise men who heralded and welcomed the child Jesus as the Messiah? Didn't Jesus' own family and disciples have greater faith than this Gentile soldier? Apparently not. What was so amazing about the centurion's faith?

What we see in the centurion is trust based upon experiential knowledge of the power in the words spoken by authorized individuals. In a personal universe, words really can direct actions and events. This is true whether we're speaking of our own small arena or God's cosmos.

REFLECT: *Whom have you known whose word you have trusted implicitly? If they said they would show up, you knew they would—even if it looked as if they wouldn't. Imagine having such trust in God, believing that he will show up, no matter what. If you trusted God that much, how would your life be different? What would you stop doing? Start doing differently?*

Effortless Obedience

"Say the word, and my servant will be healed."

LUKE 7:7

For the centurion, faith was relatively easy. Jesus said he would heal the servant, and the centurion believed it. He recognized he was dealing with someone in high authority. He had experienced people in Roman authority and how they could command an event to happen or use mere words to change events in a material universe. He recognized in Jesus such authority (or better!), so it was a simple matter for him to behave in faith in the situation.

Because Jesus himself understood his own authority, he responded easily to the centurion's statement about his servant's condition with an offer to heal. Without being asked, Jesus said, "I will go and heal him" (Matthew 8:7)—just like that! It didn't seem to be difficult or extraordinary to him. For Jesus, healing this servant would be like our saying, "Now I'll raise my hand."

Great faith, like great strength in general, is revealed by how easily it works. Most of what we call a struggle *of* faith is really the struggle to act *as if* we had faith when in fact we do not.

P R A Y : *Confess to God where you have struggled in your faith. Ask God to increase your faith, as the apostles did (Luke 17:5), and to let that faith create in you an easy obedience.*

MONDAY
Why We Don't Trust Words

> *For the word of the LORD is right and true;*
> *he is faithful in all he does.*
>
> PSALM 33:4

The centurion's simple faith that Jesus could heal his servant from a distance may strike us as naive (Luke 7:8). Our skepticism or practical atheism may emerge, and we may find ourselves saying (or silently thinking), "Things aren't like that! Words don't change a thing!"

What is it that bothers us? Why do we think that in our universe words cannot change reality? Truly we live in a universe in which reality responds to words, especially the "right and true" word of the Lord (Psalm 33:4). But our faith does not normally rise to believing it.

In part, our skepticism comes from the fact that we often speak words unaccompanied by faith and authority. Such words do not change reality the way words do that are laden with faith and spoken in fulfillment of an authoritative role.

PRAY: *What words of God (for example, in the Bible) have you doubted. "My peace I give you" (John 14:27)? "The Spirit of God lives in you" (Romans 8:9)? Then, if you're willing, say those words to God and follow them with, "But say the word and I will be healed" (or ". . . and I will be filled with peace," or ". . . and I will have the Spirit of God live in me").*

> *The leaders of Israel and the king humbled themselves*
> *and said, "The LORD is just."*
>
> 2 CHRONICLES 12:6

Although the centurion was a Roman soldier of considerable rank, he was also a good governor who sacrificed his private wealth to help his subjects. Although he was the top man, possibly, in the area of Capernaum, he was also a good man who loved his servant, who was sick to the point of death.

When the centurion sent word to Jesus, saying, "Lord, I do not deserve to have you come under my roof" (Matthew 8:8), this was both an act of humility and a courtesy. He knew that proper Jews thought that entering into a Gentile's house would defile them. So he said humbly to Jesus, "But just say the word, and my servant will be healed."

The Gentile centurion's humility resembles the humility of Judah's long-ago king Rehoboam and his leaders, who humbled themselves. Such persons contradict the idea that those with high authority are proud or pompous. Humility and authority do not exclude each other. When they occur in the same person, it's stunning to experience that person.

PRAY: *Consider why a person in authority might have good reason to be humble. Then pray about a situation in which you have a certain amount of control.*

Others Using Powerful Words

> *"Take the staff, and you and your brother Aaron gather the assembly together.*
> *Speak to that rock before their eyes and it will pour out its water.*
> *You will bring water out of the rock for the community*
> *so they and their livestock can drink."*

NUMBERS 20:8

According to the biblical record, powerful words such as those Jesus spoke *have* been given to other human beings to speak also. The words of others also effected changes in the physical universe.

In Numbers 20:8-12 we find a fascinating case study on this point. The Israelites, on their wilderness wanderings, were dying for lack of water. Moses' leadership was under violent criticism from his people. This drove Moses to prayer, as was right. Then God appeared to him, telling him to command a rock that was close by to give forth water: "Thus you shall bring water out of the rock for them" (v. 8 NRSV).

MEDITATE: *Read Numbers 20:1-11. Pick up a rock. Examine it carefully. Picture what happened inside the rock out of which water flowed (v. 8). How do you picture the gush of water (v. 11)? As a drinking fountain spout? As a waterfall? Spraying Moses?*

Speaking Underestimated

But the LORD said to Moses and Aaron,
"Because you did not trust in me enough to honor me as holy in the sight of the Israelites,
you will not bring this community into the land I give them."

NUMBERS 20:12

Instead of commanding the rock to give forth water, Moses struck it. Pretty impressive. Why did God deal sternly with him for his lack of trust? This may not seem like a serious offense unless one understands the astonishing power of words said in the authority of God.

By striking the rock Moses was possibly attempting to answer those who criticized *his* power. Or perhaps he did not believe that merely *speaking* could bring water out of a rock. Maybe he thought he had to use physical force— "must *we* bring you water out of this rock?" But the rock he struck was Christ (1 Corinthians 10:4). Because the Logos, or Word, is within creation and nature, rocks are things that might respond to words spoken with the appropriate kingdom authority and vision of faith.

PRAY: *Consider how Christ accompanied the Israelites on their treacherous journey to provide a necessity of life—water—just by speaking words. How do you need to speak to Christ today about what you (or your community) need? How have you perhaps tried to get this need met by being defensive or dramatic or relying on physical force?*

Followers Catch On

As you go, preach this message: "The kingdom of heaven is near."
Heal the sick, raise the dead, cleanse those who have leprosy, drive out demons.
Freely you have received, freely give.

MATTHEW 10:7-8

Jesus approached the transfer of the power of God's word to the words of ordinary humans carefully. Although he exercised God's power in words, could his followers also handle it? He conducted this first trial run with his twelve disciples, commissioning them to do what they had seen him do, and he sent them on their way. When they returned and reported success in acting in the power of God's word, Jesus extended the transfer of God's power further to more ordinary believers: the seventy-two (Luke 10:1). Significantly these were not his closest associates, not the best-trained troops in the army of the Lord, we might say. Yet they too returned rejoicing in the knowledge that even demons were subject to them through the name of their Master (Luke 10:17).

God reigns in his kingdom through speaking. While God is usually the speaker, he also communicates in some small measure through those who work in union with him.

PRAY: *When have you seen someone demonstrate the love or power of God when you knew they were not among "the best-trained troops in the army of the Lord"? Pray for them that they too will rejoice in being used by God.*

At that time Jesus, full of joy through the Holy Spirit, said,
"I praise you, Father, Lord of heaven and earth, because you have hidden these things
from the wise and learned, and revealed them to little children.
Yes, Father, for this was your good pleasure."

LUKE 10:21

In Luke 10:21-24, Jesus seems positively gleeful, as in no other scriptural passage. Jesus "rejoiced in the Holy Spirit" (NRSV). The Greek word used here for rejoice, *agalliao,* suggests the state of mind in which people may jump up and down with joy. Then Jesus turned aside, perhaps, for a moment of thanks to his Father.

Jesus then informed his followers that his Father had turned everything over to him—"All things have been committed to me by my Father"—and that he, Jesus Christ, was to be in charge of the revelation of the Father to humanity (v. 22). He congratulated those around him on their good fortune in being able to witness what had happened, in seeing just plain folks succeed in operating with the power of God's authoritative word. Prophets and kings had longed to see this but had not been able (vv. 23-24).

REFLECT: *Why does it make sense that God uses "just plain folks"? In what way are you "just plain folks"? How would you like to see God use you powerfully?*

MONDAY

Worldwide Kingdom Participation

*Therefore I tell you that the kingdom of God will be taken away from you
and given to a people who will produce its fruit.*

MATTHEW 21:43

The governmental rule of God reaffirmed itself *through* the actions and words of the disciples and the seventy-two, all of whom belonged to Israel. But soon God's rule and witness would be removed from Israel's *exclusive* control. Because Israel failed to fulfill their divine appointment of being the light of the world, of showing the world *how to live under God,* the kingdom of God was taken away from Israel's exclusive control. The Jews as individuals were not excluded from exercising the word of power in God's kingdom. Far from it. But this was no longer their *exclusive* role *as Jews.* The Jewish people would no longer be the sole people of God, God's official address on earth.

The story of the transfer of the kingdom from the Jews exclusively to the church is the story of the New Testament book of Acts, which begins in Jerusalem and ends in Rome. Today participation in the kingdom rule of God through union with Jesus is worldwide.

PRAY: *Pray for the kingdom of God worldwide. Keep in mind that the church is increasingly concentrated in Africa and South America. Pray that those in North America and Europe will welcome these new expressions of the kingdom of God.*

"O unbelieving generation," Jesus replied, "how long shall I stay with you?
How long shall I put up with you? Bring the boy to me."

MARK 9:19

Rarely does Jesus ever *pray* for a need brought before him. Rather he normally *addresses* it or *acts*. When a man brought his child to the disciples to be healed from a spirit that rendered him mute, they could not cast the spirit out. When the Master arrived he scolded his disciples for their inability (Mark 9:14-19). After some conversation with the child's father about the child's condition and about the father's own faith, Jesus cast the demon out with a command.

The ability to work with God is to be expected as we become more confident that reality—including the physical universe—is a *kingdom* in which God's authority as well as our personal relationship and communication with him are fundamental to the way things work.

MEDITATE: *Read Mark 9:15-27. Picture Jesus standing next to a father and witnessing the boy's dramatic convulsions. Watch Jesus converse gently with the father, yet challenge the father's faith. Feel the weight of Jesus' words to the spirit. Lean over with Jesus as he lifts the boy up. Feel the awe of the disciples and their regret that they were unable to do this marvelous thing.*

Prayer as Foundation

> *After Jesus had gone indoors, his disciples asked him privately,*
> *"Why couldn't we drive it out?"*
> *He replied, "This kind can come out only by prayer."*

MARK 9:28-29

Even though Jesus said the deaf and mute boy's problem could be addressed only through prayer, Jesus himself did not pray on this occasion. What is the explanation? Perhaps it was because Jesus was just returning from a trip to the mountains where the transfiguration had occurred. He had spent extensive time in prayer and was "prayed up," so to speak (Luke 9:29).

Yet Jesus' reply illustrates the principle that there are *degrees of power* in speaking the word of God and that prayer is necessary to heighten that power. Prayer is more fundamental in the spiritual life than is speaking a word. Prayer is the indispensable foundation for speaking a word. The role of speaking the word of God has become limited today because of a widespread lack of understanding of such "speaking," coupled with the generally low quality of the life of prayer.

PRAY: *Pray for someone you know who needs a type of healing. Express your earnest requests. Also ask God that "the eyes of your heart may be enlightened" for how he might use you in this situation (Ephesians 1:18).*

Prepared to Speak

> *In Lystra there sat a man crippled in his feet, who was lame from birth*
> *and had never walked. He listened to Paul as he was speaking.*
> *Paul looked directly at him, saw that he had faith to be healed and called out,*
> *"Stand up on your feet!" At that, the man jumped up and began to walk.*

ACTS 14:8-10

In most situations a *direct* word or action from God is required rather than from ourselves. Many are accustomed to praying for this. But sometimes *we* should speak, to say on behalf of God and in the name of Christ how things are to be. For example, at Lystra Paul spoke the redemptive word of God to a lame man (Acts 14:10).

To be "prayed up" so we are able to do this might be difficult, which is why Jesus told the disciples "this kind can come out only by prayer" about their inability to help the mute boy. Different situations call for different abilities, which we may or may not have available at the time. But we are called to *grow* into this capacity to speak with God, in the degree of power appointed by him for us individually.

PRAY: *Ask God to show you how you are being called to grow into this capacity to speak with God, in the degree of power appointed by him for us individually.*

F R I D A Y *Speaking Along with God*

> *Then Peter said, "Silver or gold I do not have, but what I have I give you.*
> *In the name of Jesus Christ of Nazareth, walk." Taking him by the right hand,*
> *he helped him up, and instantly the man's feet and ankles became strong.*
> *He jumped to his feet and began to walk. Then he went with them into the temple courts,*
> *walking and jumping, and praising God.*

A C T S   3 : 6 - 8

In the works done by the apostles of Jesus, we see them *speaking along with God.* They did not always pray for help, and they dealt with different situations in different ways. When Peter and John were confronted with the lame beggar, Peter commanded the man in the name of Jesus Christ—that is, on Jesus' behalf—to walk. Peter did not kneel down and pray for him, nor did he pass by saying, "We'll be praying for you!" He took the lame man by the hand and pulled him to his feet, putting his whole self on public display as an agent of Christ. Scary, isn't it?

M E D I T A T E : *Put yourself in Peter's place. What did he mean by "what I have" (v. 6)? How did his command to "walk" flow out of that? How did taking the man by the hand flow out of that? Imagine God using you in some way with an automatic response of compassion and power.*

Working Hand in Hand with God

Peter sent them all out of the room; then he got down on his knees and prayed.
Turning toward the dead woman, he said, "Tabitha, get up."
She opened her eyes, and seeing Peter she sat up.
He took her by the hand and helped her to her feet.
Then he called the believers and the widows and presented her to them alive.

ACTS 9:40-41

When dealing with Dorcas (Tabitha), the deceased sister "who was always doing good and helping the poor" (Acts 9:36), Peter put everyone out of the room. Did he learn this from Jesus, who did the same thing when he healed the daughter of the synagogue ruler (Matthew 9:23-25)?

Kneeling down, Peter prayed. Then he faced the body and commanded Dorcas to rise, and she returned to life. Perhaps Peter also learned from Elisha's practice when he raised the son of the Shunammite woman from the dead (2 Kings 4:32-35). Elisha was one of the greatest practitioners of kingdom rule with his God. We learn from the saints before us how to work hand in hand with God.

REFLECT: *Who in Scripture or your life experience have been "practitioners of kingdom rule with . . . God" from whom you need to learn? What could you do to examine their practice more closely? How eager are you to work hand in hand with God?*

M O N D A Y *Chants and Spells?*

*When Simon saw that the Spirit was given at the laying on of the apostles' hands,
he offered them money and said, "Give me also this ability so that everyone
on whom I lay my hands may receive the Holy Spirit."*

A C T S   8 : 1 8 - 1 9

How does speaking the word of God differ from superstition? When Moses, Jesus, Peter and Paul (or people today) exercised God's rule by speaking and acting with his word, how were their actions different from casting spells?

Superstition works from the belief that an *unrelated* activity influences the outcome of events. For example, if someone tries to cause you pain by mutilating a doll-like effigy of you, this is superstition because no real connection exists between the activity of sticking a pin in a doll and your body feeling pain.

Speaking and living the word of God differs from superstition because we do not believe that *the power involved resides in the words or actions alone.* Instead we regard the words and actions as God-ordained ways to accomplish what God wants. We enlist the personal agencies of the kingdom of God (prayer, authoritative words and so on) to achieve kingdom ends, not as tools to engineer our desired result. We are under authority, not in control.

R E F L E C T : *How do people superstitiously try to "get prayers answered" by saying or doing certain things? How is getting one's heart right (Acts 8:21) forgotten?*

"Speaking the Word," or Magic?

Peter answered: "May your money perish with you,
because you thought you could buy the gift of God with money!
You have no part or share in this ministry, because your heart is not right before God.
Repent of this wickedness and pray to the Lord.
Perhaps he will forgive you for having such a thought in your heart.
For I see that you are full of bitterness and captive to sin."

ACTS 8:20-23

Simon the sorcerer mistook the word and work of God for magic because he didn't understand how the kingdom of God worked. He offered Peter and John money if they would give him the power of the Holy Spirit and its manifestations. Simon, though apparently a believer (v. 13), did not have his heart right with God.

Living and acting from the power of God through reliance on Christ is not magical at all. Rather we understand and trust God, who helps us to cooperate with him in the world to enhance the kingdom of God.

MEDITATE: *Read Acts 8:14-24. Sense Simon's earnestness to be involved in the power of the Holy Spirit, even if it is twisted. Where has Simon gone wrong? Why is it easy to want good things but still be full of bitterness and captive to sin? Ask God to show you what you need to know about your own heart.*

Magical Religious Routines

And when you pray, do not keep on babbling like pagans,
for they think they will be heard because of their many words.

MATTHEW 6:7

Christians can use words and activities superstitiously, especially when speaking or acting without understanding how the kingdom of God functions. For example, some Christians get caught up using the phrase "what you say is what you get" (or "name it and claim it"). Supposedly if you affirm what you want, you get it. But if you say what you *do not* want—voicing something you worry might happen—that also happens to you. This *is* superstition, making us resemble those who Jesus said "heap up empty phrases as the Gentiles do" in prayer, thinking "that they will be heard because of their many words" (Matthew 6:7 NRSV).

Possibly many professing Christians have little *except* superstition in their religious activities. They pray "in Jesus' name," thinking it's almost magical but not understanding what the phrase entails. We must each search our heart on this matter. We do not have to be superstitious if we seek above all the kingdom of God.

PRAY: *Reread the last paragraph and be honest and open as you ask God to show you any ways you are superstitious about phrases you use, programs you're involved in or people you associate with. Ask forgiveness as needed and ask God to show you the way forward.*

Legalism as Superstition

For I tell you that unless your righteousness surpasses that of the Pharisees and the teachers of the law, you will certainly not enter the kingdom of heaven.

MATTHEW 5:20

Legalism claims that overt *actions* in conforming to rules for explicit behavior make us right and pleasing to God. It's as if we believe that power resides in the words or in the rituals themselves. Jesus called legalism "the righteousness . . . of the scribes and Pharisees" (Matthew 5:20).

Legalism and superstition are closely joined by their emphasis on controlling people and events through little rules, bypassing the realities of the heart and soul from which life really flows. That is why Jesus tells us we must go *beyond* the righteousness of the scribes and Pharisees to heart-and-soul transformation if we are truly to enter into life.

R E F L E C T: *In what ways do we become almost superstitious about certain practices of the faith, insisting they be done certain ways or with certain words? How are we showing faith in our own spirituality rather than in God himself?*

Playing with Power

> *One day the evil spirit answered them,*
> *"Jesus I know, and I know about Paul, but who are you?"*
> *Then the man who had the evil spirit jumped on them and overpowered them all.*
> *He gave them such a beating that they ran out of the house naked and bleeding.*

ACTS 19:15-16

What happens if words of kingdom authority are spoken without prayer, without an understanding of the kingdom or without faith, hope and love? A traveling troupe of Jewish exorcists, the seven sons of Sceva, found out. When they saw the miracles of God worked through Paul, they imitated the *words* Paul used, mistaking them for incantations rather than intelligent, rational discourse within the kingdom. The demons they tried to exorcise recognized their fakery and attacked them. (This caused believers who had been using spells to forsake magic so that the word of the Lord spread [v. 20]!)

As followers of Christ we are not to believe or act on things that make no sense. We do not try to make things work for our own ends, no matter how respected those things might be.

REFLECT: *When have you been tempted, if ever, to imitate the words or techniques of those whose faith you admire? What did you learn about needing the right heart out of which such words or actions flow? What heart change did you still need to experience?*

What Is the Word of God?

For you have been born again, not of perishable seed, but of imperishable,
through the living and enduring word of God.

1 PETER 1:23

What is the relationship between the word of God as spoken in Acts and the Bible as the Word of God? While the Bible is the written Word of God, *the word of God is not simply the Bible.* Let's look at what the Bible says about the word of God. The word includes Jesus Christ, who is the *living* Word (1 Peter 1:23) born of a virgin, crucified, resurrected and elevated to the right hand of the Father. The word of God is also that which is settled eternally in the heavens (Psalm 119:89), expressing itself in the order of nature (Psalm 19:1-4). The word of God is that which expanded, grew and multiplied in the book of Acts (Acts 12:24). None of these things are the Bible, but they *all* are God's *words,* as is also his speaking that we hear when we individually hear God.

M E D I T A T E : *Choose the idea about the word of God above that has least penetrated your thinking. Turn to the reference indicated next to it and read the verse and its context. Ponder what it would mean to more deeply regard that entity as the word of God. Close by thanking God for the "living and enduring word of God."*

M O N D A Y *The Word Working in You*

> *When you received the word of God, which you heard from us,*
> *you accepted it not as the word of men, but as it actually is,*
> *the word of God, which is at work in you who believe.*

1 THESSALONIANS 2:13

The Bible is *one* result of God's speaking. It is a finite, *written* record of the saving truth spoken by the infinite, living God. It fixes the boundaries of everything he will ever say to humankind *in principle,* though it does not provide the detailed communications that God may have with individual believers today.

The Bible is inerrant (free of errors) in its original form and infallible in all forms for the purpose of guiding us into a life-saving relationship with God in his kingdom. But this accomplishes the purposes of redemption only as we constantly hold that text within the eternal living Word. Inerrancy of the originals also does not guarantee sane, sound, error-free interpretations. As we read the Bible today, we must depend on God, who now speaks to us in conjunction with it and with our best efforts to understand it.

PRAY: *Ask God to help you hear him in the words of the Bible and to hold what you hear within the eternal living Word. Ask God to help you understand it. Ask God to show you what prayers you need to offer while reading the Bible.*

Receiving the Word of God

*The sacred writings . . . are able to instruct you
for salvation through faith in Christ Jesus. All scripture is inspired by God
and is useful for teaching, for reproof, for correction, and for training in righteousness,
so that everyone who belongs to God may be proficient,
equipped for every good work.*

2 T I M O T H Y 3 : 1 5 - 1 7 N R S V

The Bible has its own special and irreplaceable role in the history of redemption. We can refer persons to it with the assurance that if they will approach it openly, honestly, intelligently and persistently, God will meet them through its pages and speak peace to their souls.

The word of God in the larger sense portrayed *in* the Bible is therefore available to every person *through* the Bible, the written Word of God. All may hear the living Word by coming to the Bible humbly and persistently, with burning desire to find God and live in peace with him.

P R A Y : *Consider the upcoming opportunities you will have to hear God through the Bible: a personal devotional time, a friend's ideas, a sermon or a book. Pray now that in those moments you will open yourself to whatever God would say to you through the Bible—to correct you if necessary, to show you the next step in any area of life.*

Fellowship with the Living Word

Show me your ways, O LORD, teach me your paths;
guide me in your truth and teach me, for you are God my Savior,
and my hope is in you all day long.

PSALM 25:4-5

The Bible may prove a deadly snare for some as it did for those in Christ's earthly days, who actually used Scripture to dismiss him and his claims on them (John 5:36-47). Because of this we are warned in the Bible that we can twist the Scripture to destroy ourselves as some did with Paul's epistles, for "some things in them [are] hard to understand, which the ignorant and unstable twist to their own destruction, as they do the other scriptures" (2 Peter 3:16 NRSV). Our only protection from our own pride, fear, ignorance and impatience as we study the Bible is fellowship with the living Word, the Lord himself, invoked in constant supplication from the midst of his people, as we see in this stanza from the hymn "Break Thou the Bread of Life" by Mary Ann Lathbury:

O send Thy Spirit, Lord, now unto me,

That He may touch my eyes, and make me see;

Show me the truth concealed within Thy word,

And in Thy book revealed, I see thee Lord.

PRAY: *Pray Psalm 25:4-5. Pause after each phrase. Wait in quiet or expand on that phrase in prayer.*

I tell you the truth, if anyone says to this mountain,
"Go, throw yourself into the sea,"
and does not doubt in his heart but believes that what he says will happen,
it will be done for him.

MARK 11:23

Many people have difficulty accepting the more spectacular episodes of God's word at work, such as we see in Scripture. Yet the same people believe in the healing power of prayer and in the capacity of activities practiced by the church to heal the physical body.

With the return of the gifts of the Spirit to prominence across all denominational boundaries, multitudes of disciples once again dare to *speak* in the name of Jesus to needs and dangers that confront them. Also, the practice of so-called spiritual warfare has prepared countless others to "speak to the mountain," as Jesus said they might. Testimonies of remarkable results find their way into many fellowships and Christian literature. This is to be expected as *we grow in our confidence that reality—including the material world—is ultimately a kingdom in which authority, personal relationship and communication are basic to the way things run.*

REFLECT: *Which, if any, of these truths do you find difficult to believe or understand: reality is a kingdom; reality is permeated by God's authority; reality is permeated by a personal relationship with God and communication with him? Ask God to help you absorb these truths.*

When Things Don't Happen

Open up before GOD, keep nothing back;
he'll do whatever needs to be done:
He'll validate your life in the clear light of day
and stamp you with approval at high noon.

PSALM 37:5-6 *THE MESSAGE*

The suggestion that we *should* possibly heal the sick, cast out demons or raise the dead by participating in God's word and power may leave us baffled. After speaking about accomplishing things through prayer, I was confronted by a tearful, angry woman. Earlier she had believed that prayer could make a difference in life's events and had tried to make this work. When it did not, she felt hurt and guilty. To protect herself she had adjusted her faith to consist of believing the creeds, helping out at church and being a good person. Many fine people are convinced that the biblical mode of life in God's kingdom cannot be a reality for them.

When we consider a life of participating in God's kingdom rule, *we* do not have to make it happen. There is nothing forced about it. We can trust God to do the luminous works and lead us in ways that are suitable to our lives and his calling for us.

REFLECT: *Have you adjusted your faith because of disappointments about what you thought would happen in God's kingdom? In what ways have you preferred to live your life untouched by God's authority and communication?*

So-Called Failure

Do not rejoice that the spirits submit to you,
but rejoice that your names are written in heaven.

LUKE 10:20

A devout woman who had been raised in a fellowship that stressed receiving a "second work of grace" had been driven to distraction in frantic efforts to obtain this "deeper life" and cease being a second-class citizen among her religious friends. But she "failed," changed denominations and recoiled into a life of mere mental assent to the truth about Jesus. As I taught about the joyous possibilities of life by entering into God's kingdom and real interaction with God in the manner described in the Old and New Testaments, she was thrown into agony because she had supposedly failed.

As we experiment in the ways of God, we learn how he works and that he never majors in the spectacular. This is not our work. The extent of our obligation is to be honestly willing and eager to be made able. We keep in mind how Jesus told his seventy-two friends on their return from their mission that they should not rejoice in spectacular works, but that they were part of God's kingdom.

PRAY: *Review with God your "failures" to do great works in the past. Turn them over one by one and thank God for himself and for the future possibilities of real interaction with him.*

M O N D A Y *Christians as Conduits*

> *May the God of peace, who through the blood of the eternal covenant*
> *brought back from the dead our Lord Jesus, that great Shepherd of the sheep,*
> *equip you with everything good for doing his will, and may he work in us*
> *what is pleasing to him, through Jesus Christ, to whom be glory for ever and ever. Amen.*

HEBREWS 13:20-21

When those who work with the word of God have an understanding about the way the kingdom of God works and they are filled with faith, hope and love, they are *by their very nature* linked to the effect to be brought about. Their way of being forms the appropriate conduit to connect the supply of God's power to the situation requiring God's power. They form a natural (though really supernatural) path from the Great Influencer to the situation or person needing influence—that he may work in us (Hebrews 13:21).

This process occurs because the all-present, all-powerful, all-knowing divine mind of God mediates between the word spoken by his faithful servant on his behalf and the waves or rocks needing attention or the body or mind needing to be healed.

PRAY: *Ask God to prepare you to be a faithful, hopeful and loving conduit in your very nature between himself and the hard places and rough situations around you and in the world.*

Examples of God's Indwelling

You are the light of the world. A city on a hill cannot be hidden.
Neither do people light a lamp and put it under a bowl.
Instead they put it on its stand, and it gives light to everyone in the house.

MATTHEW 5:14-15

God doesn't speak only for our prosperity, safety or gratification. Those who are united with God are also fitted by him to show humankind how to live. They, and they alone, are at home in the universe. They are the light of the world—not what they do but who they *are*.

Those who receive the grace of God's saving companionship in his word, those in the Way who lead an eternal kind of life teach others how to live by *showing* them. God's work of transformation in us makes us examples of his indwelling. It communicates God's redeeming word and Spirit to other human beings. In us as in Jesus Christ himself, *the Life* is to be *"the light* of all people" (John 1:4 NRSV, emphasis added).

MEDITATE: *Read Matthew 5:14-15 and ponder it. Imagine yourself as someone out of whom love and justice flow to the extent that they "cannot be hidden." Imagine yourself not trying to be a witness, but being one just by the way the life that is in you overflows. Ask God to do this work in you and show you your part in this effort.*

Guides on How to Live

*Let your light shine before men, that they may see your good deeds
and praise your Father in heaven.*

MATTHEW 5:16

What great need there is today for light on how to live. Newspapers, radio and television update us on social and personal problems, which remain unsolved because of confusion about the fundamental causes of human happiness and misery. Solutions to these problems—from starvation to crime, economic disasters to disease—are not easy or simple. But where do people find insight on how to live?

The church, those "called-out" people of God, is empowered to stand up for wandering humanity to see how to live. Like the cloudy pillar by day and the pillar of fire by night that guided the Israelites through the desert (Exodus 13:21-22), the church can be the guide for answers. When faced with loneliness, alienation and war, the church should be—because it alone *could* be—the certified authority on how to live. God's resources are at the church's disposal. Christ is the answer to these social and personal difficulties of life. Jesus alone can resolve them.

PRAY: *Pray for the worldwide church to be a guide for answers to starvation, crime, economic disasters, disease, loneliness, alienation and war, so that others may see these "deeds and praise your Father in heaven."*

And pray in the Spirit on all occasions with
all kinds of prayers and requests.
With this in mind, be alert and always keep on praying for all the saints.

E P H E S I A N S   6 : 1 8

Disciples and friends of Jesus who have learned to work shoulder to shoulder with their Lord stand in this world as a point of contact between heaven and earth. They are a kind of Jacob's ladder by which the angels of God may ascend from and descend into human life (John 1:51; Genesis 28:12). Thus the disciple stands as an envoy or a receiver by which the kingdom of God is conveyed into every quarter of human affairs (Luke 10:1-11). This, as Hannah Hurnard so beautifully describes it in *God's Transmitters,* is the role of the intercessor:

> An intercessor means one who is in such vital contact with God and with his fellow men that he is like a live wire closing the gap between the saving power of God and the sinful men who have been cut off from that power. An intercessor is the contacting link between the source of power (the life of the Lord Jesus Christ) and the objects needing that power and life.

P R A Y : *Picture yourself as a "live wire" between the life of the Lord Jesus Christ and someone who needs his power and life. Desire earnestly to close the gap between these two.*

FRIDAY

Building the Mind of Christ

Let the same mind be in you that was in Christ Jesus.

PHILIPPIANS 2:5 NRSV

How do we come to have the mind of Christ? How do we follow in the steps of Christ, who did not threaten when made to suffer, who trusted himself to God (1 Peter 2:21-23)? It is through the action of the word of God *upon* us, *throughout* us and *with* us that we come to have the mind of Christ and thus to live fully in the kingdom of God.

This word of God is a creative and sustaining substance, an active power, not limited by space and time or physical constraints. It organizes and guides that which it is directed to by God and by people in union with God. It is what lies at the foundation of all the kinds of life and being there are. We come to have the mind of Christ by letting this word of God act upon us, throughout us and with us.

REFLECT: *In what numerous ways could you interact with the word of God to-day? Consider this question in light of the many facets of the word of God, including Jesus himself (1 Peter 1:23), the Bible, nature (Psalm 19:1-4), as well as the spoken message (Matthew 13; Acts 12:24).*

Alive to God

> *But because of his great love for us, God, who is rich in mercy,*
> *made us alive with Christ even when we were dead in transgressions—*
> *it is by grace you have been saved.*

EPHESIANS 2:4-5

To be "alive" is to have *power to act and respond in specific ways*. For example, a live cabbage has certain powers of action while a dead cabbage does not. A live cabbage cannot respond to a ball of string because of the kind of life that is in it. It is *dead* to the realm of play. Similarly a kitten playing with string cannot respond to poetry because it is dead to the realm of literature. Each is alive to one realm but dead to another.

Human beings were once alive to God, responding and interacting with God. When Adam and Eve mistrusted God, that cut them off from the realm of the Spirit and they became dead to it (as the cabbage is dead to the realm of play). To interact in God's kingdom once again, they needed an additional level of life to once again be alive to God.

MEDITATE: *Read Ephesians 2:4-5 again. Consider it an invitation to that "additional level of life." What things are mentioned that draw you to that additional level of life and make you think it's really possible?*

M O N D A Y *Recognizing God at Work*

> *Rabbi, we know you are a teacher who has come from God.*
> *For no one could perform the miraculous signs you are doing*
> *if God were not with him.*

JOHN 3:2

With these words, a respected spiritual leader of the Jews was impressed with Jesus and approached him. Thus this leader, Nicodemus, complimented Jesus, yet at the same time he complimented himself on being an insider who had the good sense to *recognize God at work.*

Jesus' reply to Nicodemus was a stinging rebuke, though it was delivered so gently that it was digestible and helpful. In effect Jesus said that Nicodemus had not the slightest idea what he was talking about. Nicodemus claimed to be able to recognize and see God at work, but Jesus said, "No one can see the kingdom of God without being born from above" (John 3:3 NRSV). Without this birth we cannot recognize God's workings: we do not possess the appropriate faculties and equipment.

MEDITATE: *Read John 3:1-5. Sympathize with Nicodemus. When have you been out of your depth, perhaps trying to impress someone? Maybe you even fell on your face because you didn't understand what was going on spiritually. Receive Jesus' gentle reproof. How does this make you want to be able to recognize when God is at work?*

An Additional Birth

Flesh gives birth to flesh,
but the Spirit gives birth to spirit.

JOHN 3:6

Human beings "born of water" (John 3:5)—experiencing physical birth—are alive in the flesh, in the biological and psychological realm of nature. But in relation to God they remain "dead in [their] transgressions and sins" and inhabit a world "without hope and without God" (Ephesians 2:1, 12). They can, however, be born a second time, "born from above" (John 3:3 NRSV).

They are born again not in the sense of *repeating* something or making a new start from the same place. Instead it is an *additional* kind of birth, whereby we become aware of and enter into the spiritual kingdom of God. Imagine an otherwise normal kitten that suddenly begins to appreciate and compose poetry. This sort of huge transition is involved in this additional birth. It is brought about by God's word and Spirit, and it is spiritual in its effects because "what is born of the Spirit is spirit" (John 3:6 NRSV).

R E F L E C T: *Consider how wildly radical it would be for a kitten to appreciate poetry. Consider some wildly radical things you might do as the additional birth of the Spirit takes hold of you: blessing longtime enemies; not bragging about achievements; volunteering in an activity you now consider too heroic to be considered.*

A Different Kind of Life

The wind blows wherever it pleases.
You hear its sound, but you cannot tell where it comes from or where it is going.
So it is with everyone born of the Spirit.

JOHN 3:8

Nicodemus was tripped up by Jesus' simple observation that without the additional birth people cannot recognize God's workings. Then Jesus explained that unless someone has had the usual birth (of water) and an additional birth (of Spirit) she or he cannot participate in God's governance, his kingdom.

Those born of the Spirit manifest a different kind of life. The spiritually born exhibit a life that has power to act and respond from an invisible spiritual realm and its powers. In natural terms people cannot explain what is happening with them, where they come from or where they go (John 3:8). But just as with the invisible wind and its effects, we recognize the presence of God's kingdom in a person by its effects in and around him or her.

PRAY: *Read John 3:6-21. Each time you come to a phrase that describes the different kind of life of the spiritually born, stop and ask God to move you into that kind of life. For example, from verse 8 you could ask God to bring great effects to the people around you wherever you go, just as the wind does.*

Effects of Additional Birth

He chose to give us birth through the word of truth,
that we might be a kind of firstfruits of all he created.

JAMES 1:18

The additional birth that brings a person to life in the kingdom of God is credited both to the *Spirit* (John 3:5-8) and to the *Word* (James 1:18). Peter described those who are alive to God as "born anew . . . through the living and enduring word of God," while James speaks of God giving "us birth by the word of truth" (1 Peter 1:23; James 1:18 NRSV). Peter and James had observed the effects of the word of God on them (through Christ) and the effects of the word of God on others (through them and the early church). Paul expressed this as a sober fact: "Faith comes from hearing the message, and the message is heard through the word of Christ" (Romans 10:17).

REFLECT: *How have you experienced additional strength or abilities of new birth through your experiences with Christ and others? How would you like to?*

Transformation by the Spirit

If we live by the Spirit, let us also be guided by the Spirit.

GALATIANS 5:25 NRSV

The gospel of Christ comes to us while we are alive biologically but dead to God. It both empowers and calls forth a response by its own power. This enables us to see and enter the kingdom of God as participants. It opens the door of the mind and enters the heart. From there it is able to progressively transform the whole personality.

As "the farmer sows the word" of the kingdom (Mark 4:14), it takes root in the heart and mind. Then a new life enters our personality and increasingly becomes *our* life as we learn to "be guided by the Spirit" and to be "one who sows to please the Spirit" (Galatians 5:25; 6:8).

PRAY: *Ask God to let his kingdom continually open the door of your mind and enter your heart so that your whole personality can be transformed. Ask God to help you continually be guided by the Spirit.*

New Creation

Neither circumcision nor uncircumcision means anything;
what counts is a new creation.

GALATIANS 6:15

Redemption—which is not only receiving the forgiveness of sins but also the reordering of one's whole self and life—is an aspect of God's creation. In fact, we are a new creation (2 Corinthians 5:17). As the word of God in creation brought forth light and life and matter, so the gospel of Christ comes to us and creates in us new life.

This new creation is the only thing that matters in our relation to God, as Paul says (Galatians 6:15). This new creation matters not only *someday* at the resurrection, but it also matters *today* because without it we have no relation to God. In this new creation we live each minute today, and from it arise all further developments of God's rule in our individual souls.

REFLECT: *What difference does it make that God creates us anew not only so that someday we can experience him face to face but also that today we can live in close relation to him? What do you need to do to be more conscious of living each minute in God's companionship?*

M O N D A Y   *Life as a New Creation*

> *Therefore, if anyone is in Christ, he is a new creation;*
> *the old has gone, the new has come!*

2 CORINTHIANS 5:17

What does it look like to live as a new creation each minute? C. H. Spurgeon describes it this way:

> As we have felt the Spirit of God operating on our hearts, we have known and perceived the power which he wields over human spirits. We know [the Spirit of God] by frequent, conscious, personal contact. We are made conscious of the presence of the Spirit of God and cognizant of the existence of souls as [tangibly as] we [experience] matter's action upon our senses. We have been *raised from the dull sphere of mere mind and matter into the heavenly radiance of the spirit-world.* Now, as spiritual [beings], we *discern spiritual things and feel the forces which are paramount in the spirit-realm.* We know that there is a Holy Ghost, for we feel him *operating upon our spirits.* (David Otis Fuller, ed., *Spurgeon's Lectures to His Students,* emphasis added)

PRAY: *Use some of the italicized phrases above to word a prayer about your life as a new creation. For example, you can thank God that the Spirit of God operates on your heart. Or you can ask to be raised from the dull sphere of mere matter into God's heavenly radiance to a greater degree.*

Therefore rid yourselves of all sordidness and rank growth of wickedness,
and welcome with meekness the implanted word that has the power to save your souls.

JAMES 1:21 NRSV

James, the brother of Jesus, uses the image of planting to illustrate the relationship of the additional life in the Spirit to our natural, fleshly life. After this additional life has been planted in us, our natural powers are not left to run their own way alongside the new life. Our natural powers are to be channeled through and subordinated to that life from above. All are redirected to spiritual ends, appointed to higher purposes, though they remain in themselves normal human powers.

Each individual personality remains in the uniqueness, beauty and goodness of its natural life. But a holy radiance rests upon it and shines through it because it is now the temple of God, the area over which the larger and higher power of God plays. An additional, spiritual life comes through the word of God as that word possesses and redirects the energies of the natural life to promote the ends of God's kingdom.

REFLECT: *How can you welcome the powerful word of God to be more deeply implanted in your life? How can you subordinate your natural abilities and powers to the higher working within you as a temple of God?*

Washed in the Word of God

*Love . . . just as Christ loved the church and gave himself up for her
to make her holy, cleansing her by the washing with water through the word,
and to present her to himself as a radiant church,
without stain or wrinkle or any other blemish, but holy and blameless.*

EPHESIANS 5:25-27

Christ, the Word of God, functions in our redemption also by *washing away* the impurities of the church. In this way we are cleansed from the clutter that has permeated our human personalities during our life away from God. These impurities and distractions do not automatically disappear at the additional birth. Instead they limit and attack both individual spiritual growth and the role intended for Christ's followers as the light of the world.

By his sacrificial death and triumphant resurrection, Jesus Christ finished welding his immediate followers into a totally new kind of social unit—the redemptive community, the living temple of the living God (Ephesians 2:21-22).

PRAY: *Thank God for the ongoing cleansing process that occurs in the washing away of impurities in the church. Ask God to cleanse you from the clutter that has permeated your personality during your life away from God.*

> *In him the whole building is joined together*
> *and rises to become a holy temple in the Lord.*
> *And in him you too are being built together*
> *to become a dwelling in which God lives by his Spirit.*

E P H E S I A N S   2 : 2 1 - 2 2

The church as a redemptive community and living temple of the living God provides an environment within which God's word can be present with such richness and power that the church *can* stand forth on the world scene as beyond all reasonable reproach. This is how the church is to fulfill its calling to be the light of the world—the haven and guide of all humanity on the earth.

This dwelling in which God lives by his Spirit helps renew our minds so we are able to "discern what is the will of God—what is good and acceptable and perfect" (Romans 12:2 NRSV). Hearing God becomes a reliably clear and practical matter for the mind that is transformed by this washing of the word.

P R A Y : *Ask that the worldwide church act as a holy temple and God's dwelling place, becoming a haven and guide for all humanity on the earth. Pray this for your local church as well.*

F R I D A Y

Not Immediately Recognizable

GOD called again, "Samuel!"—the third time!
Yet again Samuel got up and went to Eli, "Yes? I heard you call me. Here I am."
That's when it dawned on Eli that God was calling the boy.

1 SAMUEL 3:8 *THE MESSAGE*

We may mistakenly think that we would automatically recognize God's voice if *God* spoke to us. Abraham often did (Genesis 17—24), but Eli the priest had to learn. To think we will recognize God's voice without having to learn is a mistake. Perhaps we don't recognize God's voice right off because of our fallen and distorted condition. Or perhaps it's just normal in personal relations—certainly we didn't recognize the voice of whoever is now dear to us the first time we heard it. Or perhaps it is because of the gentleness with which our heavenly Father speaks to us. Whatever the reason, we must be *told* at first that God is speaking to us. Only later do we come, without assistance and confidently, to distinguish and recognize his voice as *his* voice. That ability comes only with experience.

P R A Y : *Ask God for help from the inner teacher, the Holy Spirit, in learning to recognize God's voice. Ask God also to bring to you people who can help you know that God is speaking to you. Finally, pray that in due time God will use you to help someone else recognize God's voice.*

Confusion and Mystery

> *In thee, O LORD, do I put my trust:*
> *let me never be put to confusion.*
>
> P S A L M   7 1 : 1   K J V

If we have an openness and are willing to learn, we can come to recognize the voice of God with assistance from those who are familiar with the divine voice from their own experience. On the other hand, we should understand that it is in Satan's best interest to make an *inherent mystery* of God's word coming directly to us. In this way the power of God's specific word for our lives can be hindered or lost. Without qualified help working alongside our desire to learn and readiness to cooperate, God's direct word may remain a riddle or a game of theological charades.

This is generally the condition of the church today, I suspect. This would explain why there is such great confusion and difficulty about what it really means to walk with God. Such confusion allows evil impulses to move into the vacuum and sweep us away.

R E F L E C T : *How do the following keep us from being confused and feeling as if God's voice is a mystery: seeking qualified help in hearing God's voice; a desire to learn to hear it; a readiness to cooperate with God? How can any of these lead to more confusion if not worked out with wisdom?*

MONDAY

Cleansing the Shirt's Fibers

He saved us, not because of righteous things we had done,
but because of his mercy.
He saved us through the washing of rebirth and renewal by the Holy Spirit,
whom he poured out on us generously through Jesus Christ our Savior.

TITUS 3:5-6

Think for a moment about what happens when you wash a dirty shirt: the water and laundry soap move through the fibers of the shirt material and carry out the dirt lodged within those fibers. When we come to God, our minds and hearts are like that dirty shirt, cluttered with false beliefs and attitudes, deadly feelings, past deeds, misguided plans, hopes and fears.

The word of God—primarily the gospel of his kingdom and of the life and death of Jesus on our behalf—enters our mind and brings new life through faith. As we open our entire life to this new power and to those sent by God to minister the word to us, the word moves into every part of our personality, just like the water and soap move through the shirt's fibers. God's word pushes out and replaces all that is false and opposed to his purposes in creating us and putting us in our unique place on earth.

MEDITATE: *Offer God your pieces of "dirty laundry" one by one. After naming each, read (aloud, if you wish) Titus 3:5-6.*

Washing Our Minds

> *When they hurled their insults at him, he did not retaliate;*
> *when he suffered, he made no threats.*
> *Instead, he entrusted himself to him who judges justly.*

1   P E T E R   2 : 2 3

Before we can hear God, a multitude of things must first be washed from the mind. Only the powerful and living word of God is capable of removing these obstacles. For example, we usually think that if we are mean enough to people they will be good. We hope to control people by threatening them and punishing them. We are afraid they will not think we mean what we say unless we shout. Yet this was not the way of Jesus. He let others punish him and said, "And I, when I am lifted up from the earth [on the cross], will *draw* all people to myself" (John 12:32 NRSV, emphasis added).

REFLECT: *Consider the last time you shouted or spoke severely. What were you afraid would happen, if anything? Why did anger or forceful language seem necessary? How did Jesus avoid this by "entrust[ing] himself to him who judges justly"?*

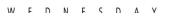

WEDNESDAY,

Who Will Serve Me?

For whoever wants to save his life will lose it,
but whoever loses his life for me will save it.
What good is it for a man to gain the whole world,
and yet lose or forfeit his very self?

LUKE 9:24-25

An untold number of false ideas and attitudes corrupt our minds and lives and must be washed out by the entry of God's word. "The unfolding of your words gives light; it gives understanding to the simple" (Psalm 119:130). Certain thought patterns need to be examined and offered to God for cleansing. For example, we are apt to believe that we must serve ourselves or no one else will. But Jesus knew that those who would save their life must lose it (Luke 9:24-25). We are pretty well convinced that we gain by grabbing and holding, but Jesus taught us, "Give, and it will be given to you" (Luke 6:38).

PRAY: *Confess to God the situations in which you are afraid you will not be helped—where you feel you must do for yourself or suffer. Ask God to help you to let go of self-protection and to become convinced that God will show up, no matter what.*

Preoccupied with God's Presence

The LORD replied,
"My Presence will go with you, and I will give you rest."

EXODUS 33:14

For many of us who profess to follow Christ, much inward change may be needed before we can hear God correctly. When trouble comes—for example, when we have car problems or get into a dispute with someone—how long does it take us to bring it to God in prayer? When we see an accident or some violent behavior or we hear an ambulance down the street, do we think to hold those concerned up to God in prayer? When we meet with a person for any reason, do we go in a spirit of prayer so that we are prepared to minister to them, or they to us? When we are alone, do we recognize that God is present with us? Does our mind spontaneously return to God when not intensely occupied, as the needle of the compass turns to the North Pole when removed from nearer magnetic sources?

MEDITATE: *Say Exodus 33:14 several times to yourself. Then picture yourself stuck because your car or bus has broken down. Repeat the verse again. Picture yourself at an upcoming social engagement (friendly lunch, family gathering) and repeat the verse again. Imagine other scenarios where you are not likely to practice the presence of God, and repeat it again.*

Needing to Be Cleansed

We wait for light, and lo! there is darkness;
and for brightness, but we walk in gloom.
We grope like the blind along a wall, groping like those who have no eyes;
we stumble at noon as in the twilight,
among the vigorous as though we were dead.

ISAIAH 59:9-10 NRSV

A recent report from a mental health clinic told how removing coffee from the waiting rooms transformed the patients' behavior. When coffee was available, patients constantly bickered and violence even occurred. After the stimulation of caffeine was withdrawn, only two or three unpleasant scenes occurred per week. Like the caffeine, poisonous thoughts, beliefs, fears, lusts and attitudes compel us to destructive behavior that we do not understand and whose source we do not recognize.

Today, with all our knowledge, technology and sophisticated research, we find our world in the same situation as that described by Isaiah many centuries before Christ. This is because our minds need to have false thoughts and habits washed out of them. They so badly need to be washed that we rarely understand what life would be like if they *were* cleaned, and many of us do not even sense the need for cleaning.

PRAY: *Confess to God times you do not understand your behavior or recognize its sources. Ask God to bring before your mind what life would be like without these destructive thoughts.*

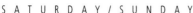

A New Character

But the fruit of the Spirit is love, joy, peace, patience,
kindness, goodness, faithfulness, gentleness and self-control.

GALATIANS 5:22-23

Through his word Christ removes the heart and mind's old routines of thought, feeling, action, imagination, conceptualization, belief, inference and puts in their place something else: *his* thoughts, *his* attitudes, *his* beliefs, *his* ways of seeing and interpreting things, *his words.* He washes out our minds, and in the place of confusion and falsehood—or hatred, suspicion and fear, to speak of emotions—he brings clarity, truth, love, confidence and hopefulness.

So where there was fear, there is hope; where there was suspicion, there is confidence; where there was hate, there is love; and all are based on a new understanding of God conveyed into us by his word. Vessels of wrath become vessels of patience and kindness. Where there was covetousness and lust, there is generosity and courteous consideration. Where there was manipulation and possessiveness, there is trust toward God and encouragement of others toward liberty and individuality. We now have the *character* to which listening for God's voice is natural.

REFLECT: *Imagine the angels' character committee meeting about you. How would they fill in these blanks? This vessel of _____ can become a vessel of _____ and _____. Where there was once _____ and _____ in the heart, with a washing of the mind there can be _____ and _____.*

MONDAY

Communication Becomes Communion

The grace of the Lord Jesus Christ, the love of God,
and the communion of the Holy Spirit be with all of you.

2 CORINTHIANS 13:14 NRSV

While communication with God would be a stretch for many, there is still more. In the progress of God's redemptive work, *communication* advances into *communion*.

Communication often occurs over a certain distance, even amidst possible opposition. We can still communicate with those with whom we are at war. God communicates with us even while we are his enemies, dead in our sins. When communication between two people rises to the level of communion, there is a distinctness but also a profound sharing of the thoughts, feelings and objectives that make up our lives. Each recognizes the thought or feeling as his or hers, while knowing with joy that the other is feeling or thinking in the same way.

REFLECT: *When, if ever, have you experienced with God the profound sharing of the thoughts, feelings and objectives that make up your life and the life of God? If you have not, when do you imagine such a thing would be most likely to occur?*

T U E S D A Y

Communion Becomes Union

It is no longer I who live, but it is Christ who lives in me.

GALATIANS 2:20 NRSV

As God's redemptive work progresses, *communion* with God advances to *union* with God. When the progression is complete we can truly say, "It is no longer I who live, but it is Christ who lives in me" (Galatians 2:20 NRSV) and "For to me, living is Christ" (Philippians 1:21 NRSV). When communion advances into union, the sense of "mine" and "thine" may often be absent. There is only "ours."

It is this union beyond communion that Paul speaks of when he says the redeemed have the mind of Christ as well as when he exhorts us to have the mind of Christ (1 Corinthians 2:16; Philippians 2:5). Jesus prays the faithful might have this same union: "that they may be one, as we are one, I in them and you in me, that they may become completely one, so that the world may know that you have sent me and have loved them even as you have loved me" (John 17:22-23 NRSV).

P R A Y : *Talk to God honestly about the topic of "union with God." Do you long for it? Does it scare you? Does it confuse you?*

*I tell you the truth, unless you eat the flesh of the Son of Man
and drink his blood, you have no life in you.*

JOHN 6:53

If the good that Christ offers us in the redeemed life is to become real in ourselves, we must appreciate the *literal* character of the Scriptures that speak of Christ's being *in* us. In what may have been his first attempt to make this plain, Jesus told his followers that they would "eat his flesh" and "drink his blood" (John 6:53-55). Those who heard these words were offended, for they did not understand that he spoke of his flesh and blood to speak of himself in the most concrete terms. He immediately explained that his actual flesh, when taken apart from his *spiritual, personal reality,* would do them absolutely no good at all (John 6:63). He goes on to describe his *words* as "spirit and life."

It was through his *words* that he literally imparted himself while he lived and taught among the people of his day. On the foundation of these words, his crucifixion, resurrection and Pentecost brought forth a communion and then a union later described by the apostle Paul as the great mystery of the ages, "Christ in you, the hope of glory" (Colossians 1:27).

MEDITATE: *Read John 6:53-55. How could you describe these words as delightful (instead of gory) when properly understood?*

Christ's Faith as Our Faith

> He got up, rebuked the wind and said to the waves, "Quiet! Be still!"
> Then the wind died down and it was completely calm.
> He said to his disciples, "Why are you so afraid? Do you still have no faith?"
>
> MARK 4:39-40

Jesus himself lived by faith in God and his kingdom. His followers did not have this faith within themselves. They regarded it only as *his* faith, not theirs. Even after they came to have faith *in him,* they did not share his faith. Once in the middle of the Sea of Galilee, the disciples' boat was almost beaten under by the waves while Jesus slept calmly. His disciples woke him crying, "Teacher, don't you care if we drown?" (Mark 4:38). After speaking powerful words to the sea, he reproachfully replied, "Why are you so afraid? Do you still have no faith?"

Didn't the disciples have faith? They called on Jesus, counting on him to save them. They had great faith in him, but they did not have *his great faith in God.* It was because they did not have *his* faith that he spoke of them having no faith.

MEDITATE: *Read Mark 4:36-39. Picture yourself as one of the disciples. Feel fear at the wind and waves and then hear Jesus' powerful words. Watch the squall die down and be amazed. Ask God to give you the faith of Christ.*

F R I D A Y

I am the vine, you are the branches.
Those who abide in me and I in them bear much fruit,
because apart from me you can do nothing.

JOHN 15:5 NRSV

The notions of "faith *in* Christ" and "love *for* Christ" leave Christ still *outside* the personality of the believer. (Are modern Bible translations being governed by the need to turn our weakened practice into the norm of faith?) These exterior notions of Christ's faith and love cannot provide the unity of the branches with the vine, where the life of the branch is literally that which flows to it through the vine and is the very life of the vine (John 15:1-4). They disallow the mutual abiding (John 15:5) that causes us branches to bring forth much fruit and without which we can do nothing. As such, abiding branches are "reconciled to [God] through the death of his Son, [so] how much more, having been reconciled, shall we be saved through his life!" (Romans 5:10).

PRAY: *Turn to John 15:1-5 (use the KJV, NKJV or NRSV, which use the word* abide). *Pray those verses. Begin with: "You, O Christ, are the vine. I am a branch. When I abide in you and you in me, I bear much fruit . . ."*

Really Alive

> *We were therefore buried with him through baptism into death*
> *in order that, just as Christ was raised from the dead through*
> *the glory of the Father, we too may live a new life.*

ROMANS 6:4

The substance of Paul's teachings about salvation is drained off when we fail to take literally his words about our union and identification with Christ. Without this his writings can be made into a "Roman Road" of doctrinal assents, by which we supposedly gain God's approval *merely* for believing what every demon believes to be true about Jesus and his work.

James S. Stewart's profound book *A Man in Christ* deals with this and corrects it:

> Everything that Paul associates with salvation—joy, and peace, and power, and progress, and moral victory—is gathered up in the one word he uses so constantly, "life." Only those who through Christ have entered into a vital relationship to God are really "alive." . . . What Paul saw with piercing clearness was that this was nothing else than the life of Christ Himself. He shared His very being with them.

REFLECT: *What is the difference between merely agreeing that certain doctrines are true and actually living "new life" in union and identification with Christ? What damage is done when people settle for the former and never move on to the latter?*

M O N D A Y   *God's Life in Us*

> *When Christ, who is your life, appears,*
> *then you also will appear with him in glory.*

COLOSSIANS 3:4

Our additional life through rebirth, though it is still our life, is also God's life in us: his thoughts, his faith, his love, all *literally* imparted to us, shared with us by his word and Spirit. That is why Paul used phrases such as "Christ who is your life" (Colossians 3:4) and "the life of Jesus" being "made visible in our bodies" (2 Corinthians 4:10 NRSV).

In *A Man in Christ*, James S. Stewart emphasized that "this life which flows from Christ into man is something totally different from anything experienced on the merely natural plane. It is a new quality of life, a supernatural quality (Romans 6:4)." This is what Paul means when he says that if one is *in* Christ, one is a new creation (2 Corinthians 5:17). This identity of the regenerate, or restarted, individual with the person and life of Christ himself turns believers into "a colony of heaven" (Philippians 3:20 Moffatt). It enables them to fulfill their call to be the light of the world, showing the world what it is really like to be alive.

MEDITATE: *Ponder Colossians 3:4, especially "Christ, who is your life." Relish the idea that Christ's life can be shared with us by his word and Spirit.*

TUESDAY

Focusing Our Whole Being

Since, then, you have been raised with Christ,
set your hearts on things above, where Christ is seated at the right hand of God.
Set your minds on things above, not on earthly things.
For you died, and your life is now hidden with Christ in God.

COLOSSIANS 3:1-3

The person who has been brought into the additional life by the creative action of the word of God now lives between two distinct realms of life and power: that of the natural or fleshly and that of the supernatural or spiritual. Even while dead in our sins and unable to interact constructively with God, we are still capable of sensing the vacuum in the natural life apart from God and of following up on the many earthly rumors about God and where he is to be found. Once the new life begins to enter our soul, however, we have the responsibility and opportunity of ever more fully focusing our whole being on it and wholly orienting ourselves toward it. This is *our* part, and God will not do it for us.

REFLECT: *What activities could a person do to focus on Christ? How can we learn to focus our entire being on the supernatural or spiritual while doing such things as moving rocks or scrubbing a floor? What practical difference might that make?*

Turning the Boat Around

I do not understand what I do.
For what I want to do I do not do, but what I hate I do.

ROMANS 7 : 1 5

In Romans 7, Paul illustrated how refocusing the whole being happens. Here he speaks of a time when he found that the impulses of his personality, solidified through lifelong training in the ways of sin, continued to move in their old patterns and not in conformity with the new life that had entered his soul when he encountered Christ. In this condition he said, "I fail to carry out the things I want to do, and I find myself doing the very things I hate" (7:15 JB).

This condition is like a boat traveling through water. The boat does not immediately shift to the direction the pilot wants at the moment he moves the rudder. There is lag time. And the boat may continue moving forward for some time while the engine is in full reverse. The pilot must learn how to *direct the boat* even though other powers move the boat and do not as such represent *his* intentions.

PRAY: *Ask God to give you wisdom and patience with yourself to keep up momentum toward focusing your whole being on God. Ask God to show you what negative attitudes work against this wisdom and what attitudes are needed to enhance this wisdom.*

The fact is, I know of nothing good living in me—living,
that is, in my unspiritual self—for though the will to do what is good is in me,
the performance is not, with the result that instead of doing the good things I want to do,
I carry out the sinful things I do not want.

ROMANS 7:18-19 JB

Despite failure, Paul chooses to identify with his new life. He *acknowledges and affirms* his union with what in himself cleaves to the good. "Not I, but sin" of Romans 7:20 ("it is *no longer I* that do it, *but sin* that dwells within me" NRSV, emphasis added) must be read alongside "not I, but Christ" of Galatians 2:20: "I am crucified with Christ: nevertheless I live; yet *not I, but Christ* liveth in me" (KJV, emphasis added). Some who say such things seek to excuse themselves from responsibility for their inner sinfulness or their sinful actions. But not Paul. Paul—like others who have come to life in Christ throughout the ages—does not excuse or accuse. He accepts the full measure of guilt. He is now concerned with how to enter into the new life to its fullest.

REFLECT: *Consider how often people say, "Nobody's perfect." What is implied by it: Nobody's perfect and so . . . ? What would be an appropriate finishing phrase for someone concerned about entering into new life with Christ?*

Choosing the Christ-Life

The death he died, he died to sin once for all;
but the life he lives, he lives to God.
In the same way, count yourselves dead to sin
but alive to God in Christ Jesus.

ROMANS 6:10-11

As men and women of the additional birth, we stand at the intersection of the merely natural (fleshly) and the spiritual. St. Thomas Aquinas coined a word to express this state: *aevum.* It is the mean between eternity and time, sharing in them both. It is two lives, two streams of awareness and power, mingling together in the individual who must choose which one he or she will truly be.

To focus on entering new life with Christ requires that we take a stand as to *who we are* in this new life, that we identify *with* the Christ-life in us and *against* the sin still present in our selves and that we settle in our will the question of who we intend to be. This is what it means to "count [ourselves] dead to sin but alive to God in Christ Jesus" (Romans 6:11).

PRAY: *Talk to God about the two lives, two streams of awareness and power, mingling together. Ask God to show you what you need to know about how to untangle them and choose more to be "alive to God in Christ Jesus."*

Setting the Will

> *Be energetic in your life of salvation, reverent and sensitive before God.*
> *That energy is God's energy, an energy deep within you,*
> *God himself willing and working at what will give him the most pleasure.*

PHILIPPIANS 2:12-13 *THE MESSAGE*

Our identification with the natural (fleshly) life or with the spiritual Christ-life in us is a *set of the will*. It is not to be discovered by examining theological treatises or even a state of mind. Is it my will to be in the old, dead life of sin? Or is it my will to be in the resurrection life of Christ, which has entered into me through the impact of God's word?

If you choose the latter, you still "work out your own salvation with fear and trembling, for it is God who is at work in you, enabling you both to will and to work for his good pleasure" (Philippians 2:12-13 NRSV). It *is* I. Yet it is *not I,* but Christ. We move beyond communication and communion toward union with him, and we have the opportunity of progressively unifying all aspects of our personalities with him so that, literally, "to me, living is Christ and dying is gain" (Philippians 1:21 NRSV).

MEDITATE: *Read again Philippians 2:13 in* The Message. *What word or phrase is your favorite? Which ones most help you "taste and see that the* LORD *is good" (Psalm 34:8)?*

MONDAY
The Written Word Around Us

All you have made will praise you, O LORD; your saints will extol you.
They will tell of the glory of your kingdom and speak of your might,
so that all men may know of your mighty acts and the glorious splendor of your kingdom.

PSALM 145:10-12

Once the life of Christ has entered into us, there are many things that we may do to increase the extent and depth of our union with him. But the proper use of the *written* Word is most central to our cooperative efforts with God toward full conformity with Christ.

The written Word may come to us in many ways. It may come through sermons, through art, through casual conversation, through dramatic performances, literature or song. All of these are important. For many centuries the contents of the Bible were present to the people of Europe through the architecture and artistry of their great cathedrals and churches. Indeed, even today, Christians who have read the Bible and know its contents well are often powerfully impacted on first seeing the content of the Bible communicated in magnificent stone and rich, sweeping stained-glass windows.

REFLECT: *Consider which of these avenues of the written Word you have paid least attention to: sermons, art, casual conversation, dramatic performances, literature or song. What is needed in a person's life to find the written Word more clearly in such avenues?*

Eager Use

Thy word is a lamp unto my feet,
and a light unto my path.

PSALM 119:105 KJV

The person who wishes to grow in grace is best advised to make a close and constant companion of *the book*—the Bible. God's speaking most commonly occurs in conjunction with study of and reflection on the Bible, the written Word of God, wherever the Bible is available. I do not mean that the Bible should be worshiped. Its uniquely sacred character is something that does not need to be exaggerated or even insisted on, because it is self-authenticating. It confirms itself to any earnest and open-minded user. For just as openness to and hunger for God leads naturally to reading the Bible, so the eager use of the Bible leads naturally and tangibly to the mind of God and the person of Christ.

PRAY: *Ask God to show you circumstances or settings or study tools that help you become hungry to read and glean from the Bible. What approaches? What attitudes? What methods? What prayers do you need to pray before entering the Word?*

Sharing God's Thoughts

I desire to do your will, O my God; your law is within my heart.

PSALM 40:8

The written Word of God is an expression of God's mind just as surely, though in a different manner, as are creation and Jesus, the living Word. As we read and study it intelligently, humbly and openly, we come increasingly to share God's mind.

This use of the Bible is not superstitious or magical, because a *natural connection* exists between a proper use of the Bible and its ideal result: union with Christ. The Bible expresses the mind of God, since God himself speaks to us through its pages. Thus we, in understanding the Bible, come to share his thoughts and attitudes and even come to share his life through his Word. Scripture is a *communication* that establishes *communion* and opens the way to *union*, all in a way that is perfectly understandable once we begin to experience it.

MEDITATE: *Examine Psalm 40:8 closely. How does the writer share God's mind? How does real union exist between God and the writer? Try on this writer's inner posture by saying this verse about yourself.*

Surrendered Reading

> *Do your best to present yourself to God as one approved by him,*
> *a worker who has no need to be ashamed,*
> *rightly explaining the word of truth.*

2 TIMOTHY 2:15 NRSV

We will be spiritually safe in our use of the Bible if we follow a simple rule: *Read with a submissive attitude.* Read with a readiness to surrender all you are—all your plans, opinions, possessions, positions. Study as intelligently as possible, with all available means, but never study merely to find the truth and especially not just to prove something. Subordinate your desire to *find* the truth to your desire to *do* it, to act it out!

Those who wish to hear the word and know the truth are often not prompted by their desire to *do* it. The light that such people find frequently proves to be their own snare and condemnation.

REFLECT: *Compose a prayer that includes the ideas of reading the Bible with a surrendered will and with intelligence. Pray that prayer and consider using it before you read the Bible each time—and even before reading the next entry in this book tomorrow.*

Praying the Scriptures

Knowledge puffs up, but love builds up.
The man who thinks he knows something does not yet know as he ought to know.
But the man who loves God is known by God.

1   C O R I N T H I A N S   8 : 1 - 3

Studying the Bible solely for knowledge will not do. In general, knowledge tends to be destructive when held by anything less than a mature personality thoroughly permeated by love and humility. That is true even in the secular areas of life. Few things are more terrifying in the spiritual arena than those who *absolutely know* but who are also unloving, hostile, proud, superstitious and fearful. Instead approach Bible reading with the same frame of mind in which you offer prayers to God. William Law comments in *The Power of the Spirit,* "Therefore the Scriptures should only be read in an attitude of prayer, trusting to the inward working of the Holy Spirit to make their truths a living reality within us."

R E F L E C T : *How does an attitude of Bible reading (figuring things out; getting something out of the reading) differ from an attitude of prayer? What prayer attitudes need to be applied to Bible reading and study? Try praying 1 Corinthians 8:1-3 by personalizing it so it states the ways you need to grow.*

Motives in Bible Reading

If I . . . can fathom all mysteries and all knowledge,
and if I have a faith that can move mountains, but have not love, I am nothing.

1 CORINTHIANS 13:2

Keep in mind that your aim in Bible reading is not to become a scholar or to impress others with your knowledge of the Bible—a dreadful trap for those aiming to be biblical. That aim will cultivate pride and lay a foundation for the petty, quarrelsome spirit so regrettably common in those outwardly identified as the most serious students of the Scriptures.

It may help to remember these words of Thomas à Kempis in *The Imitation of Christ:*

> Of what use is it to discourse learnedly on the Trinity, if you lack humility and therefore displease the Trinity? Lofty words do not make a man just or holy; but a good life makes him dear to God. I would far rather feel contrition than be able to define it. If you knew the whole Bible by heart, and all the teachings of the philosophers, how would this help you without the grace and love of God?

MEDITATE: *Read 1 Corinthians 13:2 until you've begun to absorb it. Then paraphrase with your own prideful tendencies. For example, "If . . . I memorize Bible chapters . . . but have not love, I am nothing."*

M O N D A Y

Soul Nourishment

> *I will instruct you and teach you in the way you should go;*
> *I will counsel you and watch over you.*

Every believer can be assured that the bread of life will be spread out for them in the Scriptures using a practice similar to one encouraged by Madame Guyon in her book *A Short and Very Easy Way of Prayer,* first published in 1688 in Lyons, France (now titled *Experiencing the Depths of Jesus Christ*). First, we come to the Scriptures as a part of our conscious strategy to cooperate with God for the full redemption of our life. We *desire* that his *revealed will should be true for us.*

Next, *we begin with familiar parts of Scripture,* such as Psalm 23, the Lord's Prayer, the Sermon on the Mount, 1 Corinthians 13 or Romans 8. You may think this is not a big beginning, but your aim must be only to nourish your soul on God's Word. That is why you go first to those parts of the Bible you already know. Count on your later growth and study to lead you to other parts that will be useful.

MEDITATE: *Turn to Psalm 23 (or another familiar passage). Read Psalm 32:8 above as God's promise to you. Then read each phrase in Psalm 23, asking God to nourish your soul and reveal his will for you.*

Taking Bites

> *Taste and see that the LORD is good;*
> *blessed is the man who takes refuge in him.*

PSALM 34:8

If you read the Bible, desiring that God's revealed will should be true for you, do not try to read a great deal at once. Also, read slowly. As Madame Guyon wisely counsels in *Experiencing the Depths of Jesus Christ,* "If you read quickly, it will benefit you little. You will be like a bee that merely skims the surface of a flower. Instead, in this new way of reading with prayer, you must become as the bee who penetrates into the depths of the flower. You plunge deeply within to remove its deepest nectar."

Do not hurry. Do not *dabble* in spiritual things. Give time for each stage to play itself out fully in your heart. Remember, this is not something you are doing by yourself. *Watch* and pray.

REFLECT: *Why is the metaphor of "tasting" Scripture an antidote to hurry? What else does the idea of tasting Scripture tell you about how to proceed in Bible reading (besides not hurrying)?*

Reading for Gold Stars

He has made us competent as ministers of a new covenant—
not of the letter but of the Spirit; for the letter kills, but the Spirit gives life.

2 CORINTHIANS 3:6

You may have been told that it is good to read the Bible through every year and that you can ensure this will happen by reading so many verses per day from the Old and New Testaments. If you do this you may enjoy the reputation of one who reads the Bible through each year, and you may congratulate yourself on it. But will you become more like Christ and more filled with the life of God?

It is a proven fact that many who read the Bible this way, as if they were taking medicine or exercising on a schedule, do not advance spiritually. It is better in one year to have ten good verses transferred *into the substance of our lives* than to have every word of the Bible flash before our eyes. This is an example of how "the letter kills, but the Spirit gives life" (2 Corinthians 3:6). We read to open ourselves to the Spirit.

REFLECT: *What methods of Bible reading have you used (or refused to use!) that had the effect of "the letter kills"? What attitudes, when applied to any method of Bible reading, make the reading legalistic?*

 *A Holy Meeting*

Send forth your light and your truth, let them guide me;
let them bring me to your holy mountain, to the place where you dwell.

P S A L M   4 3 : 3

If Scripture reading is part of your cooperative efforts with God toward full conformity with Christ, consider coming to your chosen passage as to a place where you will have a holy meeting with God. Read a small part of the passage and dwell on it, praying for the assistance of God's Spirit in bringing the realities expressed in Scripture *fully* before your mind and into your life.

Always ask,

- What is my life like because this is true?
- How shall I speak and act because of this?

You may wish to turn the passage into a prayer of praise or request. For a deeper treatment of the devotional use of the written Word, study the practice of *lectio divina* followed by many Christians. In order for the written Word of God to have its best effect, it should be made part of an overall plan of disciplines for the spiritual life.

M E D I T A T E : *Pray Psalm 43 to ask God's Spirit for assistance. Then use the above approach and questions to meditate on Romans 8:28-37. End with verse 37 as a declaration of triumph: "We are more than conquerors through him who loved us."*

God Speaking About Love

*In this way, love is made complete among
us so that we will have confidence on the day of judgment,
because in this world we are like him.
There is no fear in love.
But perfect love drives out fear, because fear has to do with punishment.
The one who fears is not made perfect in love.*

1 JOHN 4:17-18

Let's look at how you might read the great "God is love" passage (1 John 4:7-21) in an effort to cultivate the Christ-life in you. As you come upon verse 18, you may prayerfully dwell on the ways in which love—God's love for us, our love for him and love among people on earth—pushes fear out of all relationships. You may think of the fearless child surrounded by loving parents, of how loving neighbors give us confidence and relieve our anxieties. You may dwell on how the assurance of God's love given to us in the death of his Son suggests that we will never be beyond his care. Seek God's help in comprehending this and in seeing what your fear-free life might be like.

PRAY: *Lift your heart in praise as you realize that God's word is now speaking in you, not just at you. Thank God for how your life is, living in his kingdom.*

God Speaking About Trust

The LORD is my shepherd, I shall not be in want.
He makes me lie down in green pastures,
he leads me beside quiet waters, he restores my soul.

PSALM 23:1-3

Reading Psalm 23 helps us surrender fears and refocus our entire being on God's kingdom. First you find *information,* which you may not automatically transfer to yourself. You may say, "This was true just for David, the psalmist." But you might sense a *yearning* that it may be so, saying, "I wish the Lord were my shepherd; that the great God would have the care and attention for me that the shepherd has for his sheep!" And as you meditate on the psalm, *affirmation* may arise ("It must be so! I want it to be so!") followed perhaps by *invocation* ("Lord, make it so for me!") and then *appropriation* (the settled conviction that it *is* so, that it is a statement of fact about you).

This last movement, *appropriation* (a declaration of triumph), must not be forced or faked. The ability to make this statement will be given as you watch for God to move in your life.

MEDITATE: *Read Psalm 23. Then reread it, noting what information strikes you, what yearning arises, what affirmation of that longing occurs, what you wish to invoke from God and finally what conviction you appropriate to yourself.*

Fall

M O N D A Y

True Colaborers

> *Every part of Scripture is God-breathed and useful one way or another—*
> *showing us truth, exposing our rebellion,*
> *correcting our mistakes, training us to live God's way.*
> *Through the Word we are put together and shaped up for the tasks God has for us.*

2 TIMOTHY 3:16-17 *THE MESSAGE*

When there is an inner agreement between our minds and the truth expressed in the passages we read, we know that we have part of the mind of Christ *in us as our own.* For these great truths conveyed by Scripture were the very things that Jesus believed. They constituted the faith, hope and love in which he lived. As they become our beliefs, his mind becomes our mind. We are fitted out then to function as true colaborers with God, as brothers, sisters and friends of Jesus in the present and coming kingdom of God. And we are in a position to know and understand fully how God speaks today to his children.

REFLECT: *Which of God's tasks do you need to be more "fitted out" for? Where does your subtle rebellion need to be exposed? How do you need training to live God's way? What passage of Scripture might you meditate on that would help to equip you?*

Applied Truth

I am your servant;
give me discernment that I may understand your statutes.

PSALM 119:125

When a word or thought comes to us—through others, the inner voice, some special experience, the Bible or circumstances—*how* do we know whether or not it is a word from God to us? What about it indicates it has a divine source?

Of course, we can know that the word is from God if it corresponds with the plain statement or meaning of Scripture, understood in such a way that it is consistent with soundly interpreted biblical teaching. For example, God directs us never to worship an idol or be covetous.

Beyond this, however, the only answer to the question "How do we know whether this is from God?" is "By experience." The teachings of the Bible, no matter how thoroughly studied and firmly believed, can never by themselves constitute our personal walk with God. They have to be *applied* to us as individuals and to our circumstances, or they remain no part of our lives. We must certainly go beyond, though never *around,* the words of the Bible to find out what God is speaking to us.

PRAY: *Pray Psalm 119:125 to ask God to help you apply and understand how the truths of the Bible work themselves into your personal walk with God.*

Twisting the Word

> *A fool finds no pleasure in understanding*
> *but delights in airing his own opinions.*

PROVERBS 18:2

Even a word-for-word quotation from the Bible can be put to a use that makes it only a message from the Dear Self or from Satan. The dangers of so-called proof-texting—of taking biblical passages out of context to serve some preconceived purpose—are well known. A single statement taken directly from the Bible or statements used for personal application may be used in ways *contrary* to the purposes of God (such as saying, "I can do all things through Christ who strengthens me" when your body is overworked and needs rest), contrary to any meaning that God may have in mind for us. That is why *only the Bible as a whole* can be treated as the written Word of God.

REFLECT: *What attitudes or practices can safeguard us from using Scripture verses as proof-texts? What questions do we need to ask ourselves when we quote Scripture at ourselves?*

Voice Recognition in Nature

The ox knows his master, the donkey his owner's manger,
but Israel does not know, my people do not understand.

ISAIAH 1:3

Domesticated animals and pets recognize the voice of their master and learn to do so very quickly. Charlie Frank raised the elephant Neeta from birth and trained her as a circus performer. On retirement he gave her to the San Diego Zoo. After they had not seen each other for fifteen years, a television crew filmed their reunion. Frank called to Neeta from about a hundred yards away. She came to him immediately and performed her old routines on command. Her past experience gave her the power to recognize his voice. Humans don't always do as well as animals in voice recognition, as Isaiah noted, but they can learn to recognize the voice of God.

But humans can learn to recognize God's voice just as they learn from experience alone how to recognize the color red, with its various shades and characteristics, and to distinguish it from blue or yellow. A musician learns by experience to distinguish a minor key from a major one simply by hearing a melody. We learn by experience to recognize God's voice.

REFLECT: *What do you think causes people not to recognize God's voice? What do you think would help you learn to recognize God's voice more fully?*

True Light

The true light that gives light to every man was coming into the world.
He was in the world, and though the world was made through him,
the world did not recognize him.

JOHN 1:9-10

The light that shines on every human being who comes into the world some-times strikes the blinded eyes of fallen humanity in vain. The word that has gone out to the very ends of the earth (Psalm 19:4) falls on deaf ears. But those who have been given the additional birth—the new birth through the redemptive message of Christ that has entered their lives—can learn by experience to hear God as he speaks, to recognize his word and confidently interact with it. In *God's Perfect Will*, G. Campbell Morgan describes this recognition:

> To the individual believer, who is, by the very fact of relationship to Christ, indwelt by the Holy Spirit of God, there is granted the direct impression of the Spirit of God on the spirit of man, imparting the knowledge of his will in matters of the smallest and greatest importance. This has to be sought and waited for.

PRAY: *Thank God that Christ's true light shines on every human being. Confess any deafness to hearing his voice. Ask God to help you learn from experience to hear his voice.*

The anointing that you received from him abides in you,
and so you do not need anyone to teach you.
But as his anointing teaches you about all things,
and is true and is not a lie, and just as it has taught you, abide in him.

1   J O H N   2 : 2 7   N R S V

The apostle John learned about God's voice from experience and wrote with authority about it: "The shepherd . . . calls his own sheep by name and leads them out. . . . The sheep follow him because they know his voice" (John 10:2-4 NRSV). These words were not merely a record of what Jesus said. They also describe John's experience with Christ, his Lord and friend. John's emphasis on having seen, heard and touched the Word of Life is startling (1 John 1:1-3). In the presence of the visible, touchable Jesus, John learned to recognize when God was speaking.

In later experience John became so confident of the inner teacher that he told his children in the faith, as he warned them about deceit, that they did not need anyone other than the inner teacher, the Holy Spirit (1 John 2:27).

M E D I T A T E :   *Imagine the apostle John writing the words recorded in John 10:2-4. What do you see on his face—radiance? tears of joy?—as he remembers the voice of Christ, his Lord and friend?*

M O N D A Y *The Three Lights*

> *A matter must be established by the*
> *testimony of two or three witnesses.*
>
> DEUTERONOMY 19:15

Many discussions about hearing God's voice speak of three points of reference, also called "three lights," that we can consult in determining what God wants us to do. These are *impressions of the Spirit, passages from the Bible* and *circumstances.* When these three things point in the same direction, it is suggested, we may be sure the direction in which they point is the one God intends for us. In *The Secret of Guidance,* Frederick B. Meyer explains:

> God's *impressions within* and *his word without* are always corroborated by his *providence around,* and we should quietly wait until those three focus into one point. And when the time comes for action, circumstances, like glowworms, will sparkle along your path. (emphasis added)

It is possible to understand this precious advice in such a way that it completely resolves any problem about hearing God's voice. This is normally the case for those who have already learned to recognize the inner voice of God.

R E F L E C T : *Which of these "three lights" is most easy for you to discern? Which is most difficult? Why do you think one is easier than another for you? What, if anything, does this tell you about how God may be stretching you?*

Not a Checklist

> *But when Jesus turned and looked at his disciples,*
> *he rebuked Peter. "Get behind me, Satan!" he said.*
> *"You do not have in mind the things of God, but the things of men."*

MARK 8:33

While one may recognize in retrospect how the three lights (impressions of the Spirit, passages from the Bible and circumstances) work, trying to discern the three lights in the present may result in a swirl of confusion. Those without experience in the Way of Christ may try to use them as a formula, spiritual gimmick or quick fix—all "things of men" (Mark 8:33). They will then fall prey to the desire to get their own way and to secure their own prosperity and security. The three lights cannot be used as a checklist—trying to get a reading of what circumstances say, a separate reading of what the Bible says and yet another separate reading of what the Spirit says, as we might get an accurate reading of the time of day by consulting three different clocks.

PRAY: *Ask God to show you how you might have used spiritual tools (such as Bible reading or intercessory prayer) as gimmicks or quick fixes. Have you turned Scripture verses or principles into checklists or formulas? Ask God to show you what approaches help you "have in mind the things of God" instead.*

Working Interdependently

But if he will not listen, take one or two others along,
so that "every matter may be established by the testimony of two or three witnesses."

MATTHEW 18:16

Those experienced in the Way of Christ know it is somehow right, when trying to hear God, to look at the Bible, inner impulses of the Spirit and circumstances. None of the three lights alone is sufficient—multiple "witnesses" reveal truth (2 Corinthians 13:1; 1 Timothy 5:19).

Checking a decision against only the *Bible* can be fruitless because the Bible may have nothing to say on the topic. The veracity of a *spiritual impulse* is weighed by whether or not it confesses Jesus as Lord or Son of God (1 Corinthians 12:3; 1 John 4:2-3). Neither of these tests is helpful in practice when we are trying to decide, for example, whom to marry or which job to take. The "light" of open or closed doors of circumstances cannot function independently of the other two lights, for one does not know who is opening or closing these doors—God, Satan or another human being. These three lights correct each other. To work them out practically means realizing they are *interdependent.*

REFLECT: *Practice using the three lights. Regarding a current decision, call up these three witnesses, who have not heard each other's testimonies. Ask God to help you be open and attentive in this process.*

> My son, preserve sound judgment and discernment,
> do not let them out of your sight; they will be life for you,
> an ornament to grace your neck.

PROVERBS 3:21-22

How are we to understand the role the three lights (impressions of the Spirit, passages from the Bible and circumstances) play in hearing God's voice? Consider that a life lived by listening to God speaking is not one that excludes our own judgment. God makes full use of our mind and our will. Listening to God does not make our own decision-making process unnecessary. We ourselves, as well as others who come under the influence of God's voice, are still the ones who make the decisions.

The three lights are not a formula, but simply *factors we must consider in the process of making a responsible judgment and decision about what we are to do.* To be responsible in judgment and action is to humbly and fully consider these factors.

MEDITATE: *Chew on the words and phrases in Proverbs 3:21-22. What is the significance of preserving sound judgment? How do judgment and discernment differ? What must already be in your heart for you not to let them out of your sight? What must be in your heart for your to consider them "life" and an ornament around your neck?*

Not out of the Blue

> *Reflect on what I am saying, for the Lord will give you insight into all this.*
>
> 2 TIMOTHY 2:7

The voice of God is not itself any one of the three lights nor is it all of them together (impressions of the Spirit, passages from the Bible and circumstances). But the inner teaching of the Spirit *usually* comes to us in conjunction with responsible *study* and *meditation on the Bible*, with experience of the various kinds of *movements of the Spirit in our heart* and with intelligent *alertness to the circumstances* that befall us.

Although there are exceptions, God's directive voice does not usually come to us out of the blue. This means there are *specific, concrete things that we can do as we seek to know the will of God.* We do these things—*reflecting* on the three lights—and they turn out to be the factors in exercising responsible judgment. As we *reflect* on our circumstances, our impressions of the Spirit and passages we read in the Bible, we also *listen* for the divine voice.

MEDITATE: *Read 2 Timothy 2:1-7. Before doing so, ask the Holy Spirit to guide you. Also, bring to mind any decision or upcoming event—large or small—and set it in the back of your mind. Enjoy interacting with God as you listen to Paul's advice to Timothy.*

The Holy Spirit Speaking Today

The man without the Spirit does not accept the things that come from the Spirit of God,
for they are foolishness to him, and he cannot understand them,
because they are spiritually discerned.

1 CORINTHIANS 2:14

Some ask, "But isn't Scripture alone the one light for guidance from God?" The *Holy Spirit* works through the Scriptures to make them effective for guidance as well as redemption. Consider these comments made by William Law in *The Power of the Spirit:*

> Without the Holy Spirit, the Word of God must remain a dead letter to every man, no matter how intelligent or well-educated he may be. . . . It is just as essential for the Holy Spirit to reveal the truth of Scripture to the reader today as it was necessary for Him to inspire the writers in their day. . . . Therefore to say that, because we now have all the writings of Scripture complete, we no longer need the miraculous inspiration of the Spirit among men as in former days, is blindness. . . . In denying the *present inspiration* of the Holy Spirit, we have made Scripture the province of the letter-learned scribe. (emphasis added)

PRAY: *Hold your Bible in your hand and thank God for providing the Holy Spirit to enlighten you as you read Scripture, to bring it (and spiritual songs) to mind in the rest of life.*

MONDAY

The Weight of God's Voice

Be still, and know that I am God; I will be exalted among the nations,
I will be exalted in the earth.

PSALM 46:10

Although we learn to recognize the voice of God by experience, certain factors distinguish the voice of God, just as any human voice can be distinguished from another. The most immediate factor in the human voice, which by itself is usually enough to tell those familiar with it whose voice it is, is a certain *quality* of sound. This involves which *tones* are produced and the manner in which they are modulated. Quality, at the human level, also includes the *style* of speech. For example, is it slow or fast, smooth or halting in its flow, indirect or to the point?

The quality of God's voice is more a matter of the *weight* or impact an impression makes on our consciousness. A certain steady and calm force with which communications from God impact our soul, our innermost being, inclines us toward assent and even active compliance. The assent or compliance is frequently given before the content of the communication is fully grasped.

MEDITATE: *Experience the weight of God's words in Psalm 46:10. Close your eyes, quiet yourself and say aloud, "Be still, and know that I am God." (Pause.) "Be still, and know that I am." (Pause.) "Be still, and know." (Pause.) "Be still." (Pause.) "Be."*

The Authority of God's Voice

For he taught them as one having authority, and not as their scribes.

MATTHEW 7:29 NRSV

We sense inwardly the immediate power of God's voice. Once we have experienced it, we no longer marvel at how nature and spirits responded to this divine word in biblical examples. The unquestionable authority with which Jesus spoke to nature, humans and demons clearly manifested this quality of the word of God.

As E. Stanley Jones wrote in *A Song of Ascents*, we can distinguish the voice of God from the voice of our own subconscious because "the voice of the subconscious argues with you, tries to convince you; but the inner voice of God does not argue, does not try to convince you. It just speaks. It has the feel of the voice of God within it."

Jesus' words, weighted with authority, opened up the understanding of his hearers and created faith in them. Conversely, the authority of the scribe or the scholar comes only from his footnotes or references to someone else who is supposed to know. But God's word comes with a serene weight of authority. Because his voice bears authority within itself, it does not need to be loud or hysterical.

REFLECT: *When have you experienced authority that is serene—not bossy or loud? What was its effect on you? If you have not experienced such authority, what do you imagine would be its effects?*

This is the message we have heard from him and declare to you:
God is light; in him there is no darkness at all.

1 J O H N 1 : 5

The distinct quality of God's voice is emphasized in John Wesley's first sermon on "The Witness of the Spirit" (*Sermons on Several Occasions*), in which he posed the question of how people may know they are experiencing the "real witness" of God versus only guessing. He answers:

How do you distinguish light from darkness; or the light of a star, or a glimmering taper, from the light of the noonday sun? Is there not an inherent, obvious, essential difference between the one and the other? And do you not immediately perceive that difference? In like manner, there is an inherent, essential difference between spiritual light and spiritual darkness; and between the light [of] the Sun of righteousness and that glimmering light which arises only from "sparks of *our own* kindling."

Those practiced in recognizing God's voice immediately perceive a difference as radical as light from darkness between that divine voice and their own voice.

PRAY: *Ask God to help you recognize this distinct quality of his voice and how it differs from the voice of your subconscious mind. You may want to ask God to show you what distracts or misleads you so that his voice is not so obvious to you.*

Remarkable Effects

> *Coming to his hometown, he began teaching the*
> *people in their synagogue, and they were amazed.*
> *"Where did this man get this wisdom and these miraculous powers?" they asked.*

MATTHEW 13:54

People felt the effects of Jesus' words. They left his presence with heads and hearts full of thoughts and convictions he had authored in them through the power of God's voice and word.

I first became aware that God's word was coming to me by the effects it had on me and others around me. My main work for God is that of a teacher. I have occasionally received insights that, while perhaps of little significance in themselves, were staggering to me. Then, as I became aware and began to trust that these insights were *God's* word, I began to observe that difference between God's glowing, luminous insights and my small embers.

I also began to find that others also understood from their experience exactly what this difference was. In a 1968 *Guideposts*, Adela Rogers St. John remarked (somewhat overconfidently but to the point), "The first time you receive guidance you will know the difference. You can mistake rhinestones for diamonds, but you can never mistake a diamond for a rhinestone."

R E F L E C T : *What effects do you think would be likely to occur in people who hear words that are God's word? What thoughts might they think? What comments might they make?*

> *Jesus said, "Peace be with you!*
> *As the Father has sent me, I am sending you."*

JOHN 20:21

A certain *spirit* attaches itself to the human voice. A voice may be passionate or cold, whining or demanding, timid or confident, coaxing or commanding. This is not merely a matter of sounds but also a matter of attitudes or personal characteristics that become tangibly present in the voice.

The voice of God speaking in our souls also bears a characteristic *spirit*. It is a spirit of exalted peacefulness and confidence, of joy, of sweet reasonableness and of goodwill. It is, in short, the spirit of Jesus, and by that phrase I refer to the overall tone and internal dynamics of his personal life as a whole. (Notice Jesus' characteristic postresurrection greeting, "Peace be with you!" John 20:19, 21, 26.)

Those who had seen Jesus had truly seen the Father, who shared the same Spirit. This Spirit marks the voice of God in our hearts. Any word that bears an opposite spirit most surely is not the voice of God.

M E D I T A T E: *Say aloud the phrase, "Peace be with you!" Repeat it aloud a few more times. What spirit attaches itself to you when you say these words? Can you picture the manner with which Jesus would have said them? What facial expressions or gestures might have appropriately accompanied these words?*

> But the wisdom from above is first pure, then peaceable, gentle, willing to yield,
> full of mercy and good fruits, without a trace of partiality or hypocrisy.

JAMES 3:17 NRSV

The voice of God spoke to Bob Mumford when he was in Colombia, South America, and distinctly said, "I want you to go back to school." His description of this experience, found in his book *Take Another Look at Guidance,* brings out the quality and spirit of the voice:

> It couldn't have been any clearer if my wife had spoken the words right next to me. It was spoken straight and strong and right into my spirit. It wasn't a demanding, urgent voice. If it had been, I would immediately have suspected the source to be someone or something other than the Lord. The vocal impression was warm, but firm. I knew it was the Lord.

The sweet, calm spirit of God's voice carries over to the lives of those who speak with pure, peaceable voice. If we would heed James's words about wisdom from above, we would never lack knowledge of who speaks for God and who does not.

REFLECT: *What characteristics describe God's voice to you? Be honest. Is it chiding or gentle? Insistent or willing to yield? Scolding or full of mercy? Rehearse in your mind how each quality mentioned in James 3:17 would sound within the still, small voice of God.*

MONDAY *No Contradictions*

> *There is nothing deceitful in God, nothing two-faced, nothing fickle.*
>
> JAMES 1:17 *THE MESSAGE*

When God speaks and we recognize the voice as *his* voice, we do so because our *familiarity* with that voice enables us to recognize it. We do *not* recognize it because we are good at playing guessing games. One indicator that will help us identify that voice as God's voice is *content*. This is a matter of what information the voice conveys to us.

The content of a word that is truly from God will always conform to and be consistent with the truths about God's nature and kingdom that are made clear in the Bible. Any content or claim that does *not* conform to biblical content is not a word from God. Period! As Charles Stanley comments in *How to Listen to God*, "God's Voice will never tell us to engage in any activity or relationship that is inconsistent with the Holy Scriptures."

PRAY: *Praise God for his unchangeable nature—that who God is has been truly revealed in the Bible and that he does not change with time. Thank God that he can be counted on not to contradict himself or engage us in guessing games. Praise God as a reliable source for all things.*

TUESDAY *Nudging Us Forward*

You have stayed long enough at this mountain.
Break camp and advance. . . . I have given you this land.
Go in and take possession of the land that the LORD swore he would give to your fathers—
to Abraham, Isaac and Jacob—and to their descendants after them.

DEUTERONOMY 1:6-8

When Evan Roberts was in college studying for the ministry, he was deeply moved by the sermons of Seth Joshua, who visited his school. Roberts could not concentrate on his studies after that and went to the principal of his college, saying, "I hear a voice that tells me I must go home and speak to the young people in my home church. Mr. Phillips, is that the voice of the devil or the voice of the Spirit?" Phillips answered, very wisely, "The devil never gives orders like that. You can have a week off."

While this response, recorded by J. Edwin Orr in an article on the Welsh Revival in *The Forerunner,* may seem a little glib, it was basically right. Subsequent events in Roberts's life strongly confirmed that he was directed by the Lord on this occasion. Phillips did understand the content of the orders God is likely to give.

REFLECT: *When has God nudged you forward in ministry? Perhaps it was to help someone or to change what you were doing. Did you check with someone wiser, as Roberts did?*

Principles Are What Count

All his precepts are trustworthy.
They are steadfast for ever and ever, done in faithfulness and uprightness.

PSALM 111:7-8

In order to qualify as the voice of God, a thought, perception or other experience must conform to the principles—the fundamental truths—of Scripture. It is the *principles,* not the incidentals, of Scripture that count here. Study of the Scriptures makes clear that certain things are fundamental, absolute, without exception. They show up with stunning clarity as we become familiar with the overall content of Scripture.

For example, in 1 Corinthians 11, women are advised not to have short hair and men are informed that long hair is shameful on them. Such things are clearly *incidental.* But when you read the writings of John the apostle and learn from him "that God is light and in him there is no darkness at all" (1 John 1:5), you are on to a *principle*—something that wells up from the whole Bible and the totality of the experience of God's people through history.

P R A Y : *Ask the Holy Spirit to make clear to you what the principles of Scripture are and to let that become a guide for what you think might be the voice of God to you. Also, ask God to clear up any confusion you might have about incidentals in Scripture. Listen for God to clarify this in the next days or weeks.*

Now the Bereans were of more noble character than the Thessalonians,
for they received the message with great eagerness and examined
the Scriptures every day to see if what Paul said was true.

ACTS 17:11

Jesus tells a truly fine young man who had come to him that he must sell all he has and give the proceeds to the poor (Mark 10:21). Contrary to what many have thought, this is *incidental to people generally*, for Jesus did not ask this of everyone he met. In the particular case of this young man, Jesus' directive went right to the heart of his special problem with wealth. But it is not a principle to which all must conform. Why? Because it is not a teaching emerging from the whole of Scripture; and it should not, without further consideration and guidance, be taken as God's word to you or anyone else.

A careful student of Scripture knows the biblical *principles* regarding wealth—from Abraham to the apostle Paul—include worshiping God with offerings, using riches wisely and using them to help others. We are not to devote ourselves to gaining riches, hoarding riches or relying on them as a sense of security in life.

REFLECT: *What great harm comes from focusing on specific incidentals of Scripture rather than principles? How do we best discern principles from incidentals as careful students of Scripture?*

God's Precepts

> *The fear of the LORD is the beginning of wisdom;*
> *all who follow his precepts have good understanding.*
> *To him belongs eternal praise.*

PSALM 111:10

We discover *principles* of Scripture when we hear Jesus say that the most basic of all the commandments is "you shall love the Lord your God with all your heart, and with all your soul, and with all your mind, and with all your strength" and that the second is "you shall love your neighbor as yourself" (Mark 12:30-31 NRSV). His declaration that "those who want to save their life will lose it, and those who lose their life for my sake, and for the sake of the gospel, will save it" (Mark 8:35 NRSV) is also conveying a principle, as is his statement that we are to "strive for his kingdom, and these things will be given to you as well" (Luke 12:31 NRSV). *No specific word that is from God will ever contradict such principles.* Such principles place an ironclad restriction on what content can come with *God's* voice.

M E D I T A T E : *Turn over this sentence a few times: "All who follow his precepts have good understanding." Consider a puzzlement in your life. Ask God to show you what precepts (principles) apply to this dilemma to help you see the way forward.*

The Spirit of Jesus

What you heard from me, keep as the pattern of sound teaching,
with faith and love in Christ Jesus.

2 TIMOTHY 1:13

Principles of Scripture are to be identified most of all from the *actions, spirit* and *explicit statements* of Jesus himself. When we take Jesus in his wholeness as the model to follow (which is what it means to *trust* him), we will safely identify the content of the inner voice of God, for "whoever follows me will never walk in darkness, but will have the light of life" (John 8:12). In the awareness of this we are set free to be open to the new and special things that God wants to do in us and through us. We will be free to develop the power and authority that come from the experience of dealing directly with God— free *and* safe within the pattern of Christ's life and teachings.

PRAY: *Ask God to help you absorb the pattern of Christ's life and teachings so that when you hear God you will be able to ask yourself,* Does that sound like something Jesus would say? *and know the answer. Consider in your prayer how God might lead you to read the Gospels with regularity.*

M O N D A Y *The Spiritual Panacea*

You do not have in mind the things of God, but the things of men.

MATTHEW 16:23

Beware any voice that promises exemption from suffering and failure. This is not God's voice. In recent years spokespeople for God have used God and his Bible to guarantee health, success and wealth. If you follow these supposed guarantees, you will prosper financially, you will not get cancer, and your church will never split or lack a successful program.

The best practitioners of the Way throughout history went through great difficulties, often living their entire lives and dying amidst these trials. Recall this interchange between Jesus and Peter: "I'm going to go up to Jerusalem, and they are going to kill me," said Jesus. Peter—because he just *knew* it—replied, "Far be it from you, Lord. Such a thing shall not happen to you." Peter did not have such events in mind for himself, and hence they were not for his Messiah, the star to which he had hitched his wagon. But Jesus said to him, "Out of my sight, Satan; you are a stumbling block to me. You think as men think, not as God thinks" (Matthew 16:22-23, paraphrase).

REFLECT: *What other content involving the "things of men" rather than the "things of God" might try to pass for a voice from God? Guarantees about certain relationships? Scriptural promises of God that are skewed?*

TUESDAY

God, Not Just God's Gifts

No matter how many times you trip them up,
God-loyal people don't stay down long; soon they're up on their feet.

PROVERBS 24:16 *THE MESSAGE*

We must not be misled by wishful thinking that the Bible is a how-to manual to achieve the successful life of the Western world. The word of God does not come just to lead us out of trouble—though it sometimes does this—or to make sure that we have it easy and that everything goes our way. As disciples of Jesus, we go through the mill of life like everyone else. We are different because we *also* have a higher or additional life—a different quality of life, a spiritual life, an eternal life—*not* because we are spared the ordinary troubles that befall ordinary human beings. "For though a righteous man falls seven times, he rises again" (Proverbs 24:16).

To those living a life in conversational relationship with God, understanding how to carefully discern God's voice gives great confidence and accuracy in living day to day as the friends of Christ and as colaborers with God in his kingdom.

PRAY: *Thank God for rescuing you and walking with you through shadowy valleys. Ask God to give you confidence in living in conversational relationship with him as a friend of Christ and a partner with God in his kingdom.*

The Voice of Satan

Be self-controlled and alert.
Your enemy the devil prowls around like a roaring lion looking for someone to devour.
Resist him, standing firm in the faith, because you know that your brothers
throughout the world are undergoing the same kind of sufferings.

1 PETER 5:8-9

The voice of our adversary Satan will speak in our heart once he sees he no longer holds us in his hand. Only if we learn to recognize this voice as well can we avoid many silly attributions of events to Satan ("The devil made me do it!"). And only so can we correctly identify and firmly resist him and make him flee from us (Ephesians 6:11; James 4:7).

Satan will not come to us in the form of an oversized bat with bony wings, hissing like a snake. Very seldom will he assume any external manifestation at all. Instead he will usually, like God, come to us through our thoughts and our perceptions. We must be alert to any voice that is in contrast with the weight, spirit and content of God's voice, for that may signify that we are under subtle attack.

MEDITATE: *Focus on the phrase "standing firm in the faith." What most helps you stand firm in the faith? See yourself living this way. Why is this the best possible life for you? Does it have anything to do with being "self-controlled and alert"?*

Subtle Thoughts

Submit yourselves, then, to God. Resist the devil, and he will flee from you.
Come near to God and he will come near to you.
Wash your hands, you sinners, and purify your hearts, you double-minded.

JAMES 4:7-8

The Gospel passages do not indicate exactly how Satan came to Jesus (Matthew 4:1-11) but perhaps—and this is just a suggestion—as Jesus suffered extreme hunger, the stones around him reminded him of and even began to look like the loaves from his mother's oven. Perhaps he began to smell them and then to think how easily he could turn those stones into such loaves—with butter.

But then Jesus also realized how this vision of bread conflicted with the truth that the word of God is a substance, a meat (John 4:32). Jesus refused to allow himself to be turned away from learning that God's word is sufficient for his every need. Human beings live by every word that issues from God's mouth (Deuteronomy 8:3). The voice of temptation was clearly opposed in *spirit* and *content* to God's word, and Jesus recognized Satan and successfully resisted him in this and other temptations that followed.

REFLECT: *Which of your thought patterns typically conflict with the spirit and content of God's voice? How does Satan use subtle patterns of thought that keep you from realizing what is going on?*

Examining Thoughts

> *We demolish arguments and every pretension that*
> *sets itself up against the knowledge of God,*
> *and we take captive every thought to make it obedient to Christ.*

2 CORINTHIANS 10:5

Followers of Christ must be encouraged to believe that they can come to understand and distinguish the voice of God. They can look within their thoughts and perceptions for the same kinds of distinctions as they would find in spoken or written communications received from other human beings: a distinctive quality, spirit and content.

All of the words that we are going to receive from God, no matter what may accompany them externally or internally, will *ultimately pass through the form of our own thoughts and perceptions.* We must learn to find in them the voice of the God in whom we live and move and have our being.

MEDITATE: *Consider picturing 2 Corinthians 10:5 in a positive way. Instead of seeing yourself scolding or spanking your destructive thoughts to make them conform to Christ, see yourself exposing your darker thoughts to the "light of life" (John 8:12; see also 1:9; 1 John 1:5). Or see your broken perceptions as branches pruned from the vine and thrown away so that your fruitful thoughts can gain nourishment from the vine (John 15:1-8).*

We Are Not Infallible

Before his downfall a man's heart is proud, but humility comes before honor.

PROVERBS 18:12

Someone may ask, "When will I be sure that God is speaking to me and sure about what he says? Could I not still be mistaken, even though I've successfully heard and understood his voice many times before?" Yes, of course you could still be wrong. God does not intend to make us infallible by his conversational walk with us. You could also be wrong in believing that your gas gauge is working, that your bank is reliable or that your food is not poisoned. Such is human life. Our walk with the Lord does not exempt us from the possibility of error, even in our experienced discernment of what his voice is saying.

Infallibility, and especially infallibility in discerning the mind of God, simply does not fit the human condition. It should not be desired, much less expected, from our relationship with God.

REFLECT: *Consider why it might be so important to be infallible in discerning God's voice. How can your ability to discern God's voice become a source of pride? Is your spirituality about this ability or is it about trusting a God who is infallible?*

M O N D A Y

God's Permanent Address

> *Day after day, from the first day to the last,*
> *Ezra read from the Book of the Law of God.*
> *They celebrated the feast for seven days, and on the eighth day,*
> *in accordance with the regulation, there was an assembly.*

NEHEMIAH 8:18

If you make infallibility a condition of hearing God ("I must always hear God correctly!"), you will be discouraged. God's word is communication, and communication occurs in contexts where infallibility is out of the question. As we experiment, we grow in recognizing the word of God.

Besides, our human fallibility helps us because it forces us to maintain a close relationship with the Bible. In hearing God's voice, the written Word is central, as Ezra understood when he read it to the Jews for seven days straight. It cannot be stressed too much that the permanent address at which the word of God may be found is the Bible. More of God's speaking to me has come in conjunction with studying and teaching the Bible than with anything else. As Frederick B. Meyer wrote in *The Secret of Guidance,* "The [written] Word is the wire along which the voice of God will certainly come to you if the heart is hushed and the attention fixed."

REFLECT: *What prayer could you offer before reading Scripture to remember to hush your heart and fix your attention so that the voice of God will come?*

Our Response

> *When the king heard the words of the Book of the Law, he tore his robes.*
> *He gave these orders . . . "Go and inquire of the LORD for me and for the people*
> *and for all Judah about what is written in this book that has been found."*

2 K I N G S 2 2 : 1 1 - 1 3

Reading in the lives of the saints confirms that God's voice usually comes in conjunction with studying and teaching the Bible, as it did for King Josiah. In *Grace Abounding to the Chief of Sinners,* John Bunyan tells his story:

> One day, as I was traveling into the country and musing on the wickedness and blasphemy of my heart, and considering the enmity that was in me to God, that scripture came into my mind: "Having made peace through the blood of His cross" (Colossians 1:20). By which I was made to see, both again and again, that God and my soul were friends by his blood; yea, I saw that the justice of God and my sinful soul could embrace and kiss each other, through his blood. This was a good day to me; I hope I shall never forget it.

R E F L E C T : *How do you usually respond when spoken to by God through the Scriptures? Josiah tore his robes; John Bunyan was evidently joyful, for he said, "This was a good day to me."*

Seized by God

> *They read from the Book of the Law of God,*
> *making it clear and giving the meaning so that the*
> *people could understand what was being read.*
> *Then Nehemiah the governor, Ezra the priest and scribe,*
> *and the Levites who were instructing the people said to them all,*
> *"This day is sacred to the LORD your God. Do not mourn or weep."*
> *For all the people had been weeping as they listened to the words of the Law.*

NEHEMIAH 8:8-9

There is a huge difference between having a word of God on the page seize me and my simply seizing the words on the page (even when the study is interesting). In the former I am addressed, caught up in all the individuality of my existence by Someone beyond me. God acts toward me in a personal manner. Those across wide ranges of Christian fellowship and history, including the Jews in Nehemiah's day, have experienced this. This sense of being seized in the presence of the Scripture gives the Bible its power to assure us even though we are fallible. We stand within a community of the spoken to.

PRAY: *Ask God to help you interact with Scripture in such a way that you are addressed and seized by the words on the page. Ask that if you feel led to weep as the Jews did, you will do so freely.*

The Role of Intellectual Study

It is to be with [the king], and he is to read it all the days of his life
so that he may learn to revere the LORD his God and
follow carefully all the words of this law and these decrees and not consider himself
better than his brothers and turn from the law to the right or to the left.

DEUTERONOMY 17:19-20

Scholarship is important as a part of *our* part in responsible living before God. But intellectual study can never replace our experiencing the living voice of God. It also cannot remedy our fallibility.

In general, no person is dependent on scholarly expertise for knowledge of God. Humble openness before the recorded Word of God is sufficient for receiving his word to us. Those who *know all about* the word of God may yet never have *heard* it and recognized it. And those who have heard it and know it readily may *say* little about it. But we need many who know it and know about it to help others learn how to follow God's voice more successfully.

MEDITATE: *Read Deuteronomy 17:19-20. As you read, let God speak to you about what to emphasize more in your interaction with Scripture: reading it all the days of life; letting it teach you to revere God; praying about how to follow the teaching; not considering yourself better because you do interact with it.*

F R I D A Y

Direct Access to the Kingdom

But seek his kingdom, and these things will be given to you as well.
Do not be afraid, little flock, for your Father has been pleased to give you the kingdom.

LUKE 12:31-32

Knowing the voice of God so that we have a *practical understanding* of that voice in our minds and hearts is not a luxury for the people of God. It is not something to be allocated to those who enjoy special spiritual high points. All believers need this *direct, daily access to the kingdom of God.*

We will not receive the direction we need from the Bible *alone* or from our subjective experiences *alone* or from the interpretation of circumstances *alone.* This was never intended by God. We must be spoken to by God, specifically and concretely guided in thought and action, to the extent and through the channels he chooses.

MEDITATE: *Read Luke 12:31-32 several times. Close your eyes and picture God giving you the kingdom—as if it were a present. What do you wish to do to hold on to that present, to make it the most important thing in your life?*

Outposts of the Kingdom

Once, having been asked by the Pharisees when the kingdom of God would come,
Jesus replied, "The kingdom of God does not come with your
careful observation, nor will people say, 'Here it is,' or 'There it is,'
because the kingdom of God is within you."

LUKE 17:20-21

Understanding the voice of God gives substance to the relationship between Christ and his church. *He talks to it.* That is a major part of what it means for his word to live in the church.

When we align ourselves with the kingdom of Christ and come into the family of God, we become an outpost of that kingdom. You might say, though these are crude metaphors, that we have the telephone installed so we can take the heavenly orders and participate in decisions as we do kingdom business. We have the computer terminal put in place so we can communicate, act and interact with God in his work. It is important that we have God's instructions and directions for what we do.

PRAY: *Thank God for choosing to put the kingdom of God within you. Ask God to show you how he's talking to you as part of the church. Ask God to show you how you are to be an outpost for the kingdom in your home or work or neighborhood or place of volunteering.*

MONDAY

God's Face Turned Toward Us

The LORD bless you and keep you;
the LORD make his face shine upon you and be gracious to you;
the LORD turn his face toward you and give you peace.

NUMBERS 6:24-26

A child's mother died. He continued to be troubled, especially at night. He would come into his father's room to sleep with him. He would not rest until he knew not only that he was with his father but that his father's face was turned toward him. He would ask in the dark, "Dad, is your face turned toward me now?" And when he was assured of this, he was able to go to sleep.

How lonely life is! Many think they can get by in life with a God who does not speak. But it is not much of a life, and it is certainly not the life God intends for us or the *abundance* of life that Jesus Christ came to make available. We can have the confidence, comfort and peace that come from knowing we are indeed in communication with God himself.

MEDITATE: *Take Moses' blessing above and savor it for yourself: "The LORD blesses me and keeps me . . . makes his face to shine upon me . . . the LORD turns his face toward me . . ." Consider that this is the reality in which we live.*

God's Shining Face

Let your face shine on your servant;
save me in your unfailing love.

PSALM 31:16

Have you ever watched a child who loves her father but the father's face is continually directed away from that child—not "shining" upon her? Have you been in that place yourself? Did you experience your father's or mother's turning away from you in anger and *withdrawal*—when their faces did not shine but instead scowled at you or ignored you? Communication was cut off. You were agonized by it until you learned to harden your heart against it.

In a similar way a certain communication is absolutely necessary to our having the kind of confidence and peace appropriate to a child of God. Without real communication from God, our view of the world is impersonal, however glorious we may find God's creation. There is all the difference in the world between having a general view that this is our Father's world (or even that God has arranged for our eternal redemption) and having confidence, based in experience, that the Father's face is turned toward us, shining upon us, and that the Father is speaking to us individually.

PRAY: *Pray Psalm 31:16. First, offer the two requests. Second, thank God for answering them. Finally, thank God for being a personal, communicative God.*

"God Told Me"?

> *Turn away from godless chatter and the opposing ideas*
> *of what is falsely called knowledge.*

1 TIMOTHY 6:20

It is important for us to know on a practiced, experiential basis how God speaks so that we might protect ourselves and others about whom we are concerned. We all know what foolishness sometimes follows on the heels of the words, "God told me." Indeed, we all know what tragedies can come when people say these words.

We need to know what the voice of God is like, how it comes and what kinds of things it might say, if we are to protect ourselves and those around us in the fellowship of the faithful from people who are carried away with voices contrary to God, which they themselves may not understand.

REFLECT: *What is the best thing to say or do when someone says, "God told me," and follows it up with something that violates the spirit or content of God's voice? What are all the possible motives behind such blunders? How does that help you pray for the person?*

> *Evil men and impostors will go from bad to worse,*
> *deceiving and being deceived. But as for you, continue in what you have learned*
> *and . . . known [in] the holy Scriptures, which are able to make*
> *you wise for salvation through faith in Christ Jesus.*

2 TIMOTHY 3:13-15

If we recognize the spirit and content of God's word, we can recognize when people in positions of power and authority do not know what they are talking about. Jim Jones could have been stopped if a few of those he gathered around him could have seen through his claims to speak for God. But they had no competence in dealing with the voice of God as a practical matter. Through mystification of that voice and by "spiritual" bullying, they were literally led to the slaughter. Hearing God's voice must therefore be taken out of the realm of guesswork and put in terms everyone can understand.

If those who try to bring others under their "guidance" knew that they would be examined by compassionate but strong individuals who understand such matters, things would go much better for churches and the individuals in them.

PRAY: *Ask God to give you and the worldwide church an understanding of how he speaks, to recognize the spirit and content of his voice. Pray for the protection of the church as a whole.*

Religious Authority

> *Then we will no longer be infants, tossed back and forth by the waves,*
> *and blown here and there by every wind of teaching and by the*
> *cunning and craftiness of men in their deceitful scheming.*
> *Instead, speaking the truth in love, we will in all things grow up into him*
> *who is the Head, that is, Christ.*

EPHESIANS 4:14-15

If we are gripped by a picture of life with Jesus and moving into its reality, we will be able to resist the mistakes and abuses of religious authority, strongly but calmly. On local, national and international levels, people and groups claim to be divinely guided as to what *we* are to do. Sometimes this is correct but not always. Indeed, some leaders prefer that God speak only to them. After all, people can go off into all sorts of errors and become unmanageable once God starts "talking" to them.

Those who understand how individualized divine guidance and authority work together in Jesus' community of transforming love can respond appropriately to misuse of religious authority. Today we need people who are competent and confident in their own practice of life in Christ and in hearing his voice.

MEDITATE: *Focus on the phrase "speaking the truth in love." Imagine yourself speaking a difficult truth strongly but gently to someone who is misguided.*

"Knowing"

"We know that God spoke to Moses, but as for this fellow,
we don't even know where he comes from."
The man answered, "Now that is remarkable!
You don't know where he comes from, yet he opened my eyes."

JOHN 9:29-30

The respectable side of religion can generate dangerous responses to hearing God. When Jesus healed a blind man on the sabbath, the religious leaders "knew" that Jesus could not possibly be of God because he did not observe their sabbath restrictions about working. They "knew" the Bible and "knew" it said you were not supposed to do what Jesus did. They "knew" Jesus was a sinner. They had good, reliable general knowledge of how things were supposed to be, but they did not know *who God is* or *what his works are*. They did not recognize the greatest works of love and righteousness because those works didn't conform to their legalistic ideas of what the Bible teaches. In fact, they condemned those works. Many stand in that same place today—unable to recognize the words and works of God.

MEDITATE: *Read John 9:1-34, noting the word* know. *When have you behaved as the leaders did? When have you felt as helpless as the man explaining himself? Read verses 35-41. Put yourself in the place of the healed man. Let Jesus find you to speak to you.*

M O N D A Y *Scripture Becomes Real*

> *The LORD said to Samuel, "How long will you mourn for Saul,*
> *since I have rejected him as king over Israel? . . .*
> *I am sending you to Jesse. . . ." But Samuel said, "How can I go? . . ."*
> *The LORD said, "Take a heifer with you and say, 'I have come to sacrifice to the LORD.'"*

1   S A M U E L   1 6 : 1 - 2

Experiencing and understanding God's voice can make the Bible's events real to us and nudge our faith beyond abstract conviction to experiential reality. Our faith will grow as we identify inwardly with experiences of conversing with the Lord, such as Samuel's as he stood in the midst of Jesse's family, selecting the king over Israel. As with so much of the Bible, the passage is filled with "the Lord said to . . ."

In a normal conversational pattern, God told Samuel to go, but Samuel protested and God answered. As Jesse's sons appeared, Samuel said to the Lord that certainly this must be his choice, but God said no (vv. 6-10). When David came before Samuel, the Lord spoke again, telling him to anoint David.

MEDITATE: *Read 1 Samuel 16:1-12. Picture the events. Read aloud God's words to Samuel and hear them (vv. 1, 2, 7, 12). Stand in Samuel's shoes and imagine what it would be like to be directed so distinctly by God.*

Detailed Content

David inquired of God again, and God answered him,
"Do not go straight up, but circle around them and attack them in front of the balsam trees.
As soon as you hear the sound of marching in the tops of the balsam trees,
move out to battle, because that will mean
God has gone out in front of you to strike the Philistine army."

1   CHRONICLES   14:14-15

Ｋing David's conversational interactions with God are well documented in the Bible. In the text above, when David "inquired of God," God gave him detailed instructions for battle. It occurred just as God said.

In this and other biblical passages, God supplies *specific information*. These are not impressions, impulses or feelings, which are so commonly thought to be what God uses to communicate with us, but *clear and detailed cognitive content* concerning what is the situation, what is to be done and what will happen. David was not left to wonder if he should do this or that. He was simply told. David did not have to speculate about the meaning of "the sound of marching in the tops of the balsam trees" (v. 15); he was *told* its meaning.

M E D I T A T E : *Read 1 Chronicles 14:8-14 and imagine yourself as David hearing God marching in the tops of the balsam trees. God did just as he said! If you had been David, how would you have responded?*

Plain Communication

> *What may be known about God is plain to them,*
> *because God has made it plain to them.*

ROMANS 1:19

It is possible to talk about hearing God in terms of mysterious feelings, curious circumstances and special scriptural nuances of meaning to the point where God's character is called into question. We must reply to this tendency by stating emphatically that *God is not a mumbling trickster.*

On the contrary, it is to be expected, given the revelation of God in Christ, that if God wants us to know something (even those who "suppress the truth," Romans 1:18-19), he will be both able and willing to communicate it to us *plainly,* as long as we are open and prepared by our experience to hear and obey. This is exactly what takes place in the lives of biblical characters such as Samuel, David and so many others.

REFLECT: *Have you had moments in which you've thought of God as a mumbling trickster—even complained about his so-called sense of humor? If you have (or someone you know has), what sort of thoughts need to be expressed to God in light of his desire to communicate plainly?*

God's Voice in Their Souls

No prophecy ever came by human will,
but men and women moved by the Holy Spirit spoke from God.

2 PETER 1:21 NRSV

With very little exception, the form in which "men and women [were] moved by the Holy Spirit [and] spoke from God"—we call this inspiration—was nothing more than thoughts and perceptions of the distinctive character that these people had come, through experience, to recognize as the voice of God in their own souls. The thoughts and perceptions were still *their* thoughts and perceptions. It could not be otherwise. But the thoughts and perceptions bore within themselves the *unmistakable stamp* of divine quality, spirit, intent and origination. Peter would have known and experienced this process and seems to have thought it important to tell us.

PRAY: *Thank God for Scripture writers who recognized the distinctive character of God's voice in their thoughts and perceptions. Thank God also for contemporary prophets in your life who speak forth God's truth to you. Ask God to help you offer words and encouragement that ring with divine quality, spirit, intent and origination.*

Distinguishing Voices

I say this as a concession, not as a command. . . .
To the married I give this command (not I, but the Lord) . . .
To the rest I say this (I, not the Lord) . . .

1 CORINTHIANS 7:6, 10, 12

Paul distinguishes clearly between what the Lord said through him and what he was saying on his own (vv. 10, 12). When he composed his letters under divine inspiration, he did not stop thinking or set aside his own perceptions and feelings to become an unconscious writer or mindless voice box. His thoughts and perceptions were his, *but they were God's also.* Paul recognized them as such by virtue of the distinctive character that he knew so well and worked with in utter confidence.

Like Paul, we can learn through experience to recognize the voice of God as it enters into the texture of our souls. Our faith is strengthened by this, and we are able to claim our part in the unified reign of God in his people throughout history on earth and in heaven.

REFLECT: *How skilled are you at telling which thoughts and perceptions are typical of you (and perhaps good common sense!) and which ones are different and exceptional—perhaps because they bear the obvious quality, spirit and content of God's voice? What is your next step in becoming more skilled?*

Pursue Understanding

Get wisdom, get understanding; do not forget my words or swerve from them.
Do not forsake wisdom, and she will protect you; love her, and she will watch over you.

PROVERBS 4 : 5 - 6

Discussions about hearing God may sometimes seem remote, scholarly or philosophical. But what we *do* or *do not understand* in life is crucial. This determines what we *can* or *cannot believe* and therefore *governs our behavior and action with an iron hand.* You cannot believe a blur or a blank, and the blanks in our understanding can be filled in only by careful instruction and hard thinking. It will not be done on our behalf.

Many in our culture will tell you that hard thinking isn't necessary in the religious life. Perhaps you have seen the book titled *The Lazy Man's Guide to Riches.* Misunderstandings about faith and grace lead people to think that the Christian gospel is *The Lazy Person's Guide to Getting into Heaven When You Die* or perhaps *The Passive Person's Path to Paradise.* But it is not.

Commitment is not sustained by confusion but by insight. The person who is uninformed or confused will inevitably be unstable and vulnerable in action, thought and feeling.

MEDITATE: *Ponder Proverbs 4:5-6 and its six commands. Where have you been tempted to be lazy in your understanding or to swerve from God's truth? How would gaining understanding protect you?*

M O N D A Y   *God's Effort or Ours?*

For the LORD gives wisdom,
and from his mouth come knowledge and understanding.

PROVERBS 2:6

People of faith sometimes think knowledge is unimportant because they think they should have faith instead of knowledge. But having faith is not the opposite of having knowledge. *Faith and knowledge work together.* (Instead the opposite of living by faith is living only by sight.) People of faith often misunderstand grace as well. They think grace is the opposite of effort and since they are "saved by grace," they should not make effort. *God's grace and our effort work together.* (The opposite of grace is earning.)

To put these ideas together, then, we *make an effort* to "work out [our] salvation with fear and trembling," but in *grace* "it is God who works in you to will and to act according to his good purpose" (Philippians 2:12-13). It's right that we are to *make the effort* to "get understanding" (Proverbs 4:5, 7), yet it is by *grace* that "the LORD gives wisdom, and from his mouth come knowledge and understanding" (2:6).

P R AY : *Use the words of Proverbs 2:6; 4:5, 7 (and Philippians 2:12-13 if you wish) to pray. Ask God to help you get understanding—even to want to make the effort to gain knowledge of him. Thank God for giving wisdom, knowledge, understanding and grace.*

Diligent Students

> *Love the Lord your God with all your heart and with all your soul*
> *and with all your mind and with all your strength.*

MARK 12:30

Misunderstandings, mental confusions and mistaken beliefs about communications between God and his creatures make a strong walk with God impossible. I have repeatedly seen dire consequences of refusing to consider thoughtfully the ways God chooses to deal with us and instead relying on whimsical ideas and popular misconceptions.

Indeed, when we refuse to make the effort to understand God's dealings with humanity or to study the Bible and whatever may help us understand it, we rebel against the express will of God. For God commands us to love him with *all our mind* as well as with all our heart, soul and strength (Mark 12:30; compare Proverbs 1—8). We can therefore say on scriptural grounds that it is the will of God that we *study* his ways of communicating with us. Rejecting this thoughtful, careful study is not faith, and it does not spring from faith. It is the rejection of the God-appointed means to God-appointed goals.

REFLECT: *What do diligent students of God do when they don't understand something about God? What makes a person a diligent student of God but not puffed up with knowledge? What joy is a diligent student of God likely to experience?*

Filtering the Message

> *For this people's heart has become calloused;*
> *they hardly hear with their ears, and they have closed their eyes.*
> *Otherwise they might see with their eyes, hear with their ears,*
> *understand with their hearts and turn, and I would heal them.*

MATTHEW 13:15

Study of personal relationships shows that recognizing a certain voice is often a cue for someone to *stop* listening because they don't wish to listen to that person. Or recognizing the voice may be a cue to distort the message according to patterns in the relationship between the people involved. I am convinced that this often happens in the divine-human conversation, especially when God speaks to those who are in rebellion against him.

Jesus alerted his hearers that they might not be using their ears simply for hearing but for other purposes as well—such as filtering and managing the message to suit their lives and purposes better. Listening is an *active* process that may select, omit from or reshape the message intended by the speaker. How we listen and how we perceive messages displays our character, our freedom and our bondages.

PRAY: *Ask God questions such as these: What do I connive to hear from you? What sort of message do I purposely overlook? Do I hear your voice in a certain way (as impatient or demanding)? See what God brings to mind throughout your day.*

> *In order that "they may indeed look, but not perceive, and may indeed listen,*
> *but not understand; so that they may not turn again and be forgiven."*

MARK 4:12 NRSV

Although many say they want to hear God, they do not in reality. Because they want to run their lives without interference from God and do not want to be converted from their habitual ways, they position themselves before God in such a way that they "listen, but not understand."

The doleful reality is that few human beings really *do* concretely desire to hear what God has to say to them. When we lack the desire to receive God's word because we believe it is the best way to live, we tend to disregard the plain directives in the Scriptures (such as sanctification from sexual uncleanness and a continuously thankful heart, 1 Thessalonians 4:3; 5:18). It is not wise to disregard these plain directives and *then* expect to hear a special message from God when we want it.

REFLECT: *Consider the centrality of wanting to be converted from our habitual ways. How does truly wanting to be a different person affect our relationship with God? How are we "using" God when we ignore his general guidance in his word but expect him to answers our inquiries?*

Only When in Trouble

> *Then they will call to me but I will not answer;*
> *they will look for me but will not find me.*
> *Since they . . . did not choose to fear the LORD, . . . they will*
> *eat the fruit of their ways and be filled with the fruit of their schemes.*

PROVERBS 1:28-29, 31

Our lack of desire to hear God is shown by how rarely we listen for his voice except when we are in trouble or faced with a puzzling decision. People who truly desire to hear God's voice will want to hear it when life is uneventful. When those who do not simply want to hear God speaking in their lives in general then want a word from God when they are in trouble, they usually cannot find it. At heart they only want to get out of trouble or to make profitable decisions. Many think of divine communication *only* as something to help them avoid trouble or make decisions.

REFLECT: *Be honest with yourself: Do you seek to hear God only under uncomfortable circumstances or when trying to make a profitable decision? Ponder what has to exist in a person who wants to hear God's voice when life is uneventful.*

Desperate Appeals

From inside the fish Jonah prayed to the LORD his God. . . .
And the LORD commanded the fish, and it vomited Jonah onto dry land.

JONAH 2:1, 10

If people try to hear God only when they're in trouble or trying to make a difficult decision, is it true to say that God will not speak to them? No, this is not true. In his mercy, God communicates with and instructs those who have strayed from the general guidance of the Word he has given as he did with Jonah. Contrary to the well-meaning words of the blind man whom Jesus healed (John 9:31), God does, on occasion, "listen to sinners," and he speaks to them as well. But this cannot be counted on as part of a *regular and intelligible plan for living in a conversational relationship with God.* Anyone who rejects the general counsels of Scripture is in fact planning not to be guided by God and cannot rely on being able to be delivered from his or her difficulties by obtaining God's input on particular occasions.

PRAY: *Practice praying about uneventful circumstances. If today is an uneventful day, tell God about your day's events and ask for guidance today (keeping in mind "answers" may come at any time during the day). If today is an eventful day, pray about the seemingly insignificant details of the day.*

M O N D A Y

Living in Harmony with God

I love those who love me, and those who seek me find me.

PROVERBS 8:17

Many people honestly desire God's word both in its own right and because God knows it is best for us. As a part of their total plan for living in harmony with God, these believers adopt the general counsels of Scripture as the framework within which they are to know his daily graces. These people will most assuredly receive God's specific words through the inner voice, to the extent that it truly is appropriate in helping them become more like Christ. There is a limit to which such guidance is appropriate, but it is true in general, as G. Campbell Morgan has written in *How to Live,* that "wherever there are hearts waiting for the Voice of God, that Voice is to be heard."

M E D I T A T E : *Savor God's words recorded in Proverbs 8:17. How is someone who loves and seeks God likely to experience his daily moments of mercy and guidance? If you wish, ask God to help you become one who loves him, one who seeks him, a heart waiting for his voice.*

Expectant and Alert

> *Happy is the one who listens to me,*
> *watching daily at my gates, waiting beside my doors.*
> *For whoever finds me finds life and obtains favor from the LORD.*

PROVERBS 8:34-35 NRSV

James Dobson has given some of the best practical advice I have heard on how someone who wants the will of God and who has a basically correct understanding of it should proceed. On a radio broadcast he once described how he does it himself: "I get down on my knees and say, 'Lord, I need to know what you want me to do, and I am listening. Please speak to me through my friends, books, magazines I pick up and read, and through circumstances.'" Such waiting is not empty, but expectant and alert.

The simplicity of this should not mislead us. When we are in a proper, well-functioning relationship with God, this is exactly what we are to do. And then we are, as Dobson says, to *listen*. This means that we should pay a special kind of attention both to what is going on within us and to our surrounding circumstances.

PRAY: *If you wish, experiment with this method. Choose something you need guidance about. It may be something as small as what topic to bring up when you meet a friend for lunch. Then offer the prayer as stated above. Wait without trying to make up answers!*

Regular Times of Listening

To them God has chosen to make known among the Gentiles
the glorious riches of this mystery, which is Christ in you, the hope of glory.

COLOSSIANS 1 : 27

It is important to observe *regular* times for listening regarding the matters that especially concern you. In *The Secret of Guidance,* Frederick B. Meyer is again helpful at this practical level: "Be still each day for a short time, sitting before God in meditation, and ask the Holy Spirit to reveal to you the truth of Christ's indwelling. Ask God to be pleased to make known to you what is the riches of the glory of this mystery (Colossians 1:27)."

If we maintain this general habit, then, when we are aware of a need for a particular word from God, we will be able to listen for it with greater patience, confidence and acuteness. Generally it is much more important to cultivate the *quiet, inward space of a constant listening* than to always be approaching God for specific direction.

MEDITATE AND PRAY: *Read Colossians 1:27 and taste these words and phrases: "riches," "mystery," "hope of glory." Then ask the Holy Spirit to reveal to you the truth of Christ's indwelling. Ask God to make known to you what is the riches of the glory of this mystery today.*

In the Meantime

> *What am I doing in the meantime, Lord?*
> *Hoping, that's what I'm doing—hoping.*
>
> PSALM 39:7 *THE MESSAGE*

Often I find it works best if after I ask for God to speak to me, I devote the next hour or so to some kind of activity that neither engrosses my attention with other things nor allows me to be intensely focused on the matter in question. Housework, gardening, driving about on errands or paying bills will generally do. I do not worry about whether or not this works. I know that it does not *have* to work, but I am sure that it *will* work if God has something he really wants me to know or do. This is ultimately because *I am sure of how great and good he is.*

Often by the end of an hour or so, there has stood forth within my consciousness an idea or thought with that peculiar *quality, spirit* and *content* that I have come to associate with God's voice. If nothing emerges by the end of an hour or so, I am not alarmed. I make it a point to *keep* listening. Very often within a day something happens through which God's voice, recognizably distinct, is heard.

REFLECT: *What would be the most suitable "in the meantime" activities for you—ones that don't require enormous attention or intense focus?*

F R I D A Y *Explaining It Away*

> *So we fix our eyes not on what is seen, but on what is unseen.*
> *For what is seen is temporary, but what is unseen is eternal.*

2 CORINTHIANS 4:18

A barrier that might hinder some people's efforts to make a life in which one hears God's voice is "the seeming unreality of the spiritual life." (See Henry Churchill King, *The Seeming Unreality of the Spiritual Life*.) Or we could call it "the overwhelming presence of the visible world."

The visible world daily bludgeons us with its things and events. They pinch and pull and hammer away at our bodies. Few people arise in the morning as hungry for God as they are for cornflakes or toast and eggs. But instead of shouting and shoving, the *spiritual* world whispers at us ever so gently. And it appears both at the edges and in the middle of events and things in the so-called real world of the visible.

God's spiritual invasions into human life seem, by their very gentleness, almost to invite us to explain them away, even while soberly reminding us that to be obsessed and ruled by the visible is death but that to give one's self over to the spiritual is life and peace (Romans 8:6).

REFLECT: *How does focusing on the unseen world result in our arising in the morning as hungry for God as for cornflakes or toast and eggs?*

Verifying What We Hear

Then Gideon said to God, "Do not be angry with me.
Let me make just one more request. Allow me one more test with the fleece.
This time make the fleece dry and the ground covered with dew."
That night God did so. Only the fleece was dry; all the ground was covered with dew.

J U D G E S   6 : 3 9 - 4 0

When a thought or idea comes to me that bears the marks of God's voice, I often write it down for further study. I may also decide to discuss the matter with others, usually without informing them that "God has told me . . ." Or I reconsider the matter by repeating the same process after a short period of time. Remember Gideon and his "one more request" (Judges 6:39). Remember too that scientists check their results by rerunning experiments. We should be so humble.

I have followed this informal method of verifying what I believe I've heard from God in many situations—in university teaching, research and administration; in family and business affairs; in writing and conducting sessions in conferences and seminars. It's not a formula or legalism, just a way of conversing with God.

P R A Y : *Ask God to show you how you might experiment with something you believe he has told you. Write it down or ask God whom you might discuss the matter with.*

M O N D A Y

Guidance Comes

> *The LORD will guide you always;*
> *he will satisfy your needs in a sun-scorched land and will strengthen your frame.*
> *You will be like a well-watered garden, like a spring whose waters never fail.*

ISAIAH 58:11

From my own experience and from what I have been able to learn from the Scripture and from others who live in a working relationship with God's voice, I am led to the following conclusion: Direction will always be made available to the mature disciple if without it serious harm would befall others involved or the cause of Christ.

I believe the obedient, listening heart, mature in the things of God, will in such a case find the voice plain and the message clear, as those friends of God in the Bible did. This claim must be tested by experience, and anyone willing to meet the conditions and learn from failures as well as successes can put it to the test. In every congregation we need a group of people who, in front of everyone, are explicitly learning and teaching about life in dialog with God.

MEDITATE: *Relish the words and images of Isaiah 58:11. How do they describe someone who has an obedient, listening heart that is mature in the things of God?*

> *Then [the man in the vision] continued, "Do not be afraid, Daniel.*
> *Since the first day that you set your mind to gain understanding and to*
> *humble yourself before your God, your words were heard,*
> *and I have come in response to them."*
>
> DANIEL 10:12

Do not be misled into thinking there is some sure-fire *technique* for squeezing what you want to know out of God. What is important is a *life surrendered to God* (as Daniel exhibited), a *humble openness* to his direction even when it is contrary to our wants and assumptions, *experience* with the way his word comes to us and *fervent but patient requests* for guidance.

These do not constitute a method for getting an answer from him. Talk of method is, strictly speaking, out of place, although there are general, practical guidelines. God is not someone we "butter up" for a result, even though certain behaviors are more or less appropriate before him. We must beware of trying to *force* God to speak, especially when we are not in peaceful union with him.

REFLECT: *In what respect do you need further development: surrendering to God; opening yourself humbly to direction that may be contrary to your wants; gaining more experience with the way God's word comes to us; offering fervent but patient requests for guidance?*

Forcing a Word from God

Samuel said, "What have you done?"
Saul replied, "When I saw that the people were slipping away from me,
and that you did not come within the days appointed . . .
I said, 'Now the Philistines will come down upon me at Gilgal,
and I have not entreated the favor of the LORD';
so I forced myself, and offered the burnt offering."

1 SAMUEL 13:11-12 NRSV

A scene from King Saul's life illustrates the folly of trying to force a word from God. Saul's highest priority was not *waiting upon God to see his will done.* To keep control over his armies, he sacrificed without waiting for Samuel the priest to arrive. He blundered ahead on his own, even though it was not his place, and made offerings (1 Samuel 13:5-10).

When Samuel asked Saul why he had sacrificed without him, Saul's reply goes to the heart of his character. Saul was a man who would *take things into his own hands to get his way* and would also find a "good reason" for doing so. Samuel announced that Saul would lose his kingdom for God would not stand by such a man (vv. 11-14).

PRAY: *Confess to God times that you have taken things into your own hands (or wanted to) for "good reasons." Ask for forgiveness and further wisdom to wait upon him to see his will done.*

Celestial Aspirin?

Samuel said to Saul, "Why have you disturbed me by bringing me up?"
"I am in great distress," Saul said. "The Philistines are fighting against me,
and God has turned away from me. He no longer answers me, either by prophets or by dreams.
So I have called on you to tell me what to do."

1 SAMUEL 28:15

When Saul was facing death, he inquired of the Lord, but the Lord did not answer him (1 Samuel 28:6). As was his way, Saul tried to *force* the knowledge he sought. Even though he had banned witches from Israel, he sought out a witch and compelled her to call up the spirit of the deceased Samuel to tell him what to do (vv. 7-11). When Samuel rose "up out of the ground" (v. 13) Saul and poured out his tale of woe, saying, *"Tell me what to do"* (emphasis added).

How typical this is of the human view of God and his guidance. We treat God like a celestial aspirin that will cure headaches brought on by our willful tendencies. We treat God as a cosmic butler who cleans up our messes.

PRAY: *Pray for Christians who use God to clean up their messes. Ask God to show you how to become a disciple and friend of Jesus who has learned to work shoulder to shoulder with your Lord.*

FRIDAY *No Mysterious Catch*

You are forgiving and good, O Lord, abounding in love to all who call to you.

PSALM 86:5

Even if our hearts are attuned to God's will, there will be many times when God does not send a particularized word. We must not assume this means we are displeasing God. It is crucial to remember that God does not play hide-and-seek games with us. God is not frivolous or coy; he will not tease or torture us. With God there is no mysterious catch, no riddle to solve, no incantation to get just right—not with the God and Father of our Lord Jesus Christ!

God *is* the kind of person Jesus revealed him to be. Such a person will show us if there's a problem and what it is, provided that we openheartedly pray and seek to be shown. We must make a point of not thinking of God in terms of human beings (relatives, supervisors, authorities and others) who may have enjoyed tricking us by not explaining what we were supposed to do.

MEDITATE: *Read Psalm 86:5 again. When have you not experienced goodness from those who might have offered it, and so now you suspect God of not being good? How is God's goodness rich and full (never ending, dependable, unwavering)?*

Am I Displeasing God?

Examine yourselves to see whether you are in the faith; test yourselves.

2 CORINTHIANS 13:5

We must resolutely resist the tendency to blame the absence of a word from God automatically on our own wrongness. However, if you sincerely suspect you are the hindrance, ask God to inform you, in whatever way he chooses, if some hindrance is within you. Be quiet and listen in the inner forum of your mind for an indication that you are blocking his word. But do not endlessly pursue this. In prayer, set a specific length of time for the inquiry about hindrances: normally no more than three days. Believe that if a problem exists, God will make it clear to you.

Then take counsel from at least two people whose relationship with God you respect, preferably those who are *not* your buddies. If you find a cause for why God's word could not come, correct it. Mercilessly. Whatever it is. Just do it.

PRAY: *If you wish, ask God to show you if there is some hindrance in you that keeps you from hearing God or from God giving you direction (for example, relying on desperate appeals, listening for God only in times of trouble, disregarding God's plain directions or trying to force a word from God). Otherwise, pray for others who are seeking guidance to know if they are being hindered in some way.*

M O N D A Y *Our Character Revealed*

I the LORD test the mind and search the heart,
to give to all according to their ways, according to the fruit of their doings.

JEREMIAH 17:10 NRSV

One of the major reasons why a specific word may not be forthcoming to us in a particular case is that, in general, it is God's will that *we ourselves should have a great part in determining our path through life.* This does not mean that God is not with us. Far from it. God *develops* and, for our good, *tests* our character by letting us decide. He calls us to responsible citizenship in his kingdom by saying as often as possible, "My will for you in this case is that *you decide on your own.*" That robust and powerful saying, "I live! Yet not I, but Christ liveth in me!" (Galatians 2:20 KJV) shows that the individual human personality is not obliterated, but rather it is given its fullest expression. In most cases God does *not* run over us.

REFLECT: *Consider how much God respects the human will ("heart" in Scripture) and rarely overrides it. How has God been developing, testing and training you to make choices in life—especially recently?*

Who We Are

"If you decide that it's a bad thing to worship GOD,
then choose a god you'd rather serve—and do it today." . . .
The people answered, "We'd never forsake GOD! Never!"

JOSHUA 24:15-16 *THE MESSAGE*

The essence of human personality as God has ordained it is that it is given its fullest expression in Christ and has a great part in determining our path through life. Children cannot develop into responsible, competent human beings if they are always told what to do. Personality and character are directed from within. This inner directedness is perfected in redemption. Moreover, a child's character cannot be known—even to himself—until he is turned loose to do what he wants. It is precisely what he wants and how he handles those wants that both reveal and make him the person he is.

What we want, what we think, what we decide to do when the word of God does not come (or when we have so immersed ourselves in him that his voice within us is not distinct from our thoughts and perceptions)—these show *who we are:* either we are God's mature children, friends and coworkers, or we are something less.

REFLECT: *Consider a decision that is before you—large or small. Which choice involves motives of love, joy or peace? Which choice will develop in you more humility, kindness and self-control?*

Spiritual Hypochondria

Do not be overrighteous, neither be overwise—why destroy yourself?

ECCLESIASTES 7:16

There is a neurotic, faithless and irresponsible seeking of God's will: a kind of spiritual hypochondria, which is always taking its own *spiritual temperature,* which is far more *concerned with being righteous* than with loving God and others and doing and enjoying what is good. One can be overrighteous. We may insist on having God tell us what to do because we live in fear or are obsessed with *being right* as a strategy for *being safe.* But we may also do it because we do not really have a hearty faith in his gracious goodwill toward us. If so, we need to grow up to Christlikeness, and nothing short of that will solve our problem. Certainly more words from God will not!

PRAY: *Talk with God about how you might be overrighteous or overly concerned with how spiritual you are or aren't. Ask God to show you when you are trying to impress him or others or are overly concerned about being right. Confess as needed. Then ask God to help you simply love him and others and enjoy doing what is good.*

God Is Good

> *For the LORD is good and his love endures forever;*
> *his faithfulness continues through all generations.*

PSALM 100:5

We may be afraid to make a move without dictation from God because we suspect that he is mean and tyrannical. Far from honoring God, such an attitude is blasphemous and prevents us from entering into a conversational relationship with God, who gives sensible words, clearly revealed and reliably understood. How much would you have to do with a person who harbored such low opinions about you?

We cannot be groveling robots or obsequious, cringing sycophants and also be the children of God! Such creatures could never bear the family resemblance. A son or daughter is not their father's toady, and bootlicking does not come from humility or worship before the God and Father of Jesus Christ. To suppose so is to live within a morbid and anti-Christian view of who God is: good, loving, faithful.

MEDITATE: *Go over the key phrases in the verse above: "good," "love endures forever," "faithfulness." What morbid statements do you wish to banish from your thoughts (for example, "God must be fed up with me because . . ." or "God just wants to teach me a lesson . . .")? After each morbid statement, say this verse back to God: "For you, O LORD, are good . . ."*

F R I D A Y   *The Perfect Will of God*

If you then, though you are evil,
know how to give good gifts to your children,
how much more will your Father in heaven give
the Holy Spirit to those who ask him!

L U K E   1 1 : 1 3

If no specific word comes on an important matter such as which school to attend, where to live or what job to take, does this mean that we cannot be in God's perfect will? Are we doomed to follow an anxiety-ridden guessing game about God's will?

Assuredly it does not! Think of it this way: no decent parents would obscure their intentions for their children. A general principle for interpreting God's behavior toward us is that God will exceed us immeasurably as parents (Luke 11:13). When God gives no guidance, it is because it is *best that he does not.* Then his perfect will is whatever lies within his moral will and whatever we undertake in faith. It is no less perfect because it was not specifically dictated by him. Indeed, it is perhaps more perfect because he *trusts us to choose,* and he *goes with us in our choice.*

R E F L E C T : *Do you really believe that when God gives no guidance, it is best that he does not? Can you accept that God's will for your life is no less perfect because it was not specifically dictated by him? Think over decisions you have made. How do these ideas fit?*

> *So then, just as you received Christ Jesus as Lord,*
> *continue to live in him, rooted and built up in him,*
> *strengthened in the faith as you were taught,*
> *and overflowing with thankfulness.*

COLOSSIANS 2:6-7

God does not have an ideal, detailed life-plan designed for each believer that must be discovered in order to make correct decisions. Gary Friesen writes in *Decision Making and the Will of God* that the concept of an "individual will of God" cannot be established by reason, experience, biblical example or biblical teaching. Several courses of action may be God's perfect will for those walking in his general will. In these cases various things would equally please God.

The degree and maturity of our faith are manifested in cases where no specific command is given. Such a faith "attempts great things for God and expects great things from God" (in the words of William Carey, as he went out to India as a pioneer missionary). It actively gets on with the *work to be done* and the *life to be lived*, confident in the *good-hearted companionship of the Father, Son and Holy Spirit.*

MEDITATE: *Read Colossians 2:6-7 slowly. What words or phrases stand out to you? What do you need to know about God's general will for your life today? How can you overflow with thankfulness regarding the choices you have made about vocation, residences and so on?*

M O N D A Y

Caught in Cosmic Conflict

And we know that in all things God works for the good of those who love him,
who have been called according to his purpose. . . .
For I am convinced that neither death nor life, neither angels nor demons,
neither the present nor the future, nor any powers, neither height nor depth,
nor anything else in all creation, will be able to separate us from
the love of God that is in Christ Jesus our Lord.

ROMANS 8:28, 38-39

Sometimes we find ourselves without God's specific communication because we are face to face with the powers of darkness in the universe battling us as we share in God's activity. In these moments we stand alone as Jesus did in the hour of darkness (Luke 22:53). In that hour he cried out, "My God, my God, why have you forsaken me?" (Matthew 27:46).

You and I will face these hours too, though, I believe, we will never be *actually* forsaken and alone. No matter how well we know his voice, words from God will not spare us times of grief and pain, as Jesus was not spared. Our confidence remains that these times also "work together for good."

REFLECT: *How does mention of the powers of darkness affect you? If you say Romans 8:38-39 aloud, how deeply are you able to mean those words? Try to say them as a firm affirmation.*

The Crucible of Soul Making

In all these things we are more than conquerors
through him who loved us.

ROMANS 8:37

Sometimes we are given a word from God and are sure of it, but the events indicated do not come to pass. This is often because others involved may not know the will of God or may not do it. And God may not override them. Our world is the crucible of soul making, in which we can still remain certain of inevitable triumph, "more than conquerors." The will of God made plain to *us* is sometimes not fulfilled because of the choices of *other* people. We must not, because of that, lose confidence in God's guiding words.

PRAY: *Review with God those requests you have prayed for many years, which have not turned out as you wished (or as you believe God wishes). Consider that others may not have cooperated. Ask God to show you ways in which you are "more than a conqueror" in spite of this disappointment.*

And now these three remain: faith, hope and love.
But the greatest of these is love.

1 C O R I N T H I A N S 1 3 : 1 3

Faith, hope and love are greater than always knowing the right thing to do or always being directed by the hand of God. Knowledge and prophecy are only partial and incomplete goods (1 Corinthians 13:1-3). Faith, hope and love—truly inseparable from each other, when properly understood—are the three greatest things.

Even in Christ's hour of darkness, faith, hope and love remained with him. They always remain with us. The great height in our development as disciples of Christ is not that we always hear God's voice but that we are trained under God's hand (which includes hearing God speak and guide) in such a way that we are able to stand at appointed times and places in faith, hope and love *even without a word from God:* "and having done everything, to stand firm" (Ephesians 6:13 NRSV). We will then, as Brother Lawrence advised in *Practicing the Presence of God,* "not always scrupulously confine ourselves to certain rules, or particular forms of devotion, but act with a general confidence in God, with love and humility."

M E D I T A T E : *Read 1 Corinthians 13:13. In what appointed times and places are you being called to stand firm in faith, hope and love? Use this verse as a prayer that faith, hope and love will abide in you.*

> *Not only so, but we also rejoice in our sufferings,*
> *because we know that suffering produces perseverance;*
> *perseverance, character; and character, hope.*
> *And hope does not disappoint us, because God has poured out his love*
> *into our hearts by the Holy Spirit, whom he has given us.*

ROMANS 5:3-5

To develop toward maturity we must venture out and be placed at risk, for *only risk produces character.* This truth is intensified regarding our walk with God. In this I disagree with certain wise people who regard God's guidance as *precluding* risk. Supposedly God's guidance eliminates all risks. The immaturity of many Christians today is due to this attitude.

People even try to *use* their ability to hear God to secure a life without risk. When it does not work—as it will not—we attack ourselves, someone else or even God for being a failure. Such a response partly explains why humanity is so often disappointed with God. Who does not have a grievance against him? In truth, we need not seek risk, but we will never be without it, at least in this world. Nor should we try to be.

PRAY: *Ask God to show you when you have used him to eliminate risk, to focus only on your safety or to make your life more convenient. Ask God to build your trust in him so that you will not use him for your advantage.*

F R I D A Y   *The Larger Life*

> When Jesus spoke again to the people, he said, "I am the light of the world.
> Whoever follows me will never walk in darkness,
> but will have the light of life."

J O H N   8 : 1 2

The key concept underlying our entire journey together in hearing God is this: Hearing God's word will never make sense except when it is *set within a larger life of a certain kind*. For those in this larger life, their life will be *theirs*—preciously so—and yet also God's life; and through them will flow God's life, which is also theirs. This is the life that has its beginning in the additional birth and its culmination in the everlasting, glorious society of heaven.

To try to locate divine communication within human existence isolated from God is idolatry, where God is there for our *use*. To try to solve all our life's problems by getting a word from the Lord is to hide from life and from the dignity of the role God intended us to have in creation. We exist to stand up with God and count for something in his world.

R E F L E C T: *When we stop reducing God to only a problem solver and instead long for the larger life of Christ, "the light of life," how are these activities affected: witnessing, church advertising, church programming for adults?*

So whether you eat or drink or whatever you do,
do it all for the glory of God.

1 CORINTHIANS 10:31

We must ultimately move *beyond* the question of hearing God and into a life greater than our own—that of the kingdom of God. Our concern for discerning God's voice must be overwhelmed by our worship and adoration of him and in our delight with his creation and his provision for our whole life.

Our aim in such a life is to identify all that we are and all that we do with God's purposes in creating us and our world. Thus we learn how to do all things to the glory of God (1 Corinthians 10:31; Colossians 3:17). That is, we come to think and act in all things so that God's goodness, greatness and beauty will be as obvious as possible—not just to ourselves but also to all those around us.

PRAY: *Use phrases above to word prayers of request for help to move into a life greater than your own; to be overwhelmed by worship of God; to delight in God's creation; to think and act so that in all things God's goodness, greatness and beauty will be as obvious.*